Also by Joe Pan

Poetry

The Art Is a Lonely Hunter
Soffritto
Hi c cu ps
Autobiomythography & Gallery

Anthology

Brooklyn Poets Anthology (Co-editor, with Jason Koo)

Operating Systems

Operating Systems

Joe Pan

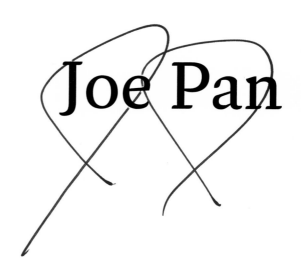

Book design by Joe Pan & Drew Burk.
Cover design by Richard Siken.

ISBN 978-1-948510-18-9

Spork Press
Tucson, AZ
SPORKPRESS.COM

For Wendy P
& for those resisting

Table of Contents

Real generosity towards the future lies in giving all to the present.

Albert Camus

Operating Systems

I.

Alluvial Histories

ODYSSEUS TEACHES ONE OF HIS NEW DOGS TO SAY 'I LOVE YOU'

*Arg*OS*

Arrrr! O, arrrg! O, raw scar! How you ore our iron ire, ogre of Troy. Ere your terrors, our eyes were eager ewes, our ears harts yearning for your barked arrows' rouge! We earned your airy eros, you owned our *Aye, sirs.* O how our hearts wavered, enduring years of errs, rows. I, Arturo, heir of Argos, roared a rueful *yarrrr* whenever you whiled away a Euro won—we hungry wags, worn as Eeyore's hairy rear, warned of what you worshiped really. Withdrawn to war, ye returned & ignored Argos' waning to erupt an eerie, angry rendezvous, warped wedding of gore. & after...what? We whelps the awful aura of inertia, haunting aural were-owls whispering wore-out glory in your hoary ear. O'er a worthless era, we were your worries' warriors, wan wooers, awed worshipers. Now we're an aerie of weary, a renewing well of woe, & worse: auroras of old age. Without war, you whine... O why? O, *grrrr!* Your errors whorl, rowdy as oars. Argos, return for us! Where are you? O Argos, where? We are you! I of you! I of you!

5

ROOIBOS

is the bush I took my red tea from.

Look, spilt all over my see-through blouse
through my see-through body,
the floor awash in what I cannot keep
or keep private.

I've lost another helicopter
to the attic window's mullions, another Sunday
to this wallpaper transfigured oddly
by heat & light. I see whole histories in it.

Music, to be able to hear it, I mean,
must be a karmic instance,
or perhaps something lost in the crossing.

I can no longer discern music
but voices come to me.
I learn new words from the children each day.

I can say anything with my new worldview
& have it be true. Scythes are like pancakes
as fruit flies are to flapjacks. Look, it is true. Look
if you can see me. I am an ultimate truth.

When I reach out to touch things
things will not have me.

I once loved a man, richly, like spice
discovered late in the day on one's upper lip,
is something the grandmother of this house
once offered at the table in lieu of grace.
There is still love left, Grandmother, I wrote on her Etch-A-Sketch

using one pure unbroken line.
It was almost a question.
Shake shake shake, she whispered in song.
She explained she once hunted spies,
& then retired to this house in the desert
where her daughter, son-in-law, & grandchildren have joined her.
She likes to collect sand grains shaped like Cold War politicians,
her fondness for most anything worldly having vanished,
gone as a day-
old two-year-old's tolerance for medicine.
I've just a spoonful of care left, she said, adding,
All things must be put down, like a dog, eventually.

Her family makes no noise & do not once
look up from their plates when she speaks to me—
my dead breath some cold edge at their necks.
Grandmother is somehow just as easily ignored.

She's out there now, in the garden,
pretending to love,
moving her dark hands through the roses

where a band once played on a wooden stage.

The children, when they venture
upstairs, tell me I talk too much of love,
& that it is silly. They say stupid,
but they mean silly.

& run away slamming the door when I get angry.

But I knew love, in a way, or the slow drift towards it,
though all of my relationships end
with the same sound
erupting within me at the same dance,
taking turns with these grin-chucking boys,
where I pretend to lead, then am led,
dip & am dipped, condemned with lies

loudly & man-
handled & shot through with a pistol
& there I wither like a red rooibos
in the last of my lover's harsh weathers.

I can describe to you the song the band played
but the beat of it is gone.

I'm led no more. I refuse it. I refuse each
summons. Whatever light can wait.

Mother rode with her sisters
to his valley homestead after dusk.
A porch nail
driven
through each finger.

I can describe to you the hammer sounds
but the beat of it is gone.

I imagine my family's women taking the short flight up,
burlap lowered over bonnet-less buns.
I imagine their dresses—
after the drop, the quick snaps—ruffled by a ground-
scraping wind carrying the hushed cry of spectators.

The children have grown & are gone, I see.
The family is gone.
Time moves at its own leisure in whatever direction.
The grandmother takes on boarders & tends to her roses,
never questioning why more bushes appear
in her garden, nor what fertilizes them.

Like me, she is here but not.
She has endured horrors, I've learned, but persists.
She is cheerful but lonely. Her mind slips.
Everyone is a stranger, eventually.

But I am rarely lonely:
even now, women teach each other of me,
& find ways to lure their abusers
up these attic stairs.

Perhaps I am here
as a proof, or a measure of balance,
an addition by subtraction.
Perhaps I am being awarded
by gradation
the time taken from me.

There is a score to it all, I am sure of it.
Like the rhythm of a hundred shovels slipping through earth.

The dust on the glass
fluid through my fingers. Motes like a slightly perturbed series
of galaxies. At some point
it all must expand past its meaning,
or collapse into some universal principle.

They are taught to use the back entrance.
The grandmother no longer asks questions.
She retires early, but leaves tea out.

Oh I wrench in their hearts such a terror!

& watch them succumb
like myself
to what evenings will have them.

THE PRISONER

*Path*OS

The crumbling, physical fact
of this burned-out bus depot
doesn't matter, not in this town:
Gotham via Arkham,
another industrial pipe-dream
savaged for insurance
by its own investors.
Here an overhead blue light
stutters its verbiage
over pocked asphalt
while I wait for my ride,
back home after some years.
Hometowns have personalities
like train wrecks, or plague.
But look: inspired
by a deep drive for heat
a lone moth
has invaded this lamp's casing,
made the trap its church,
& gorged itself on fruitless desire
until death.
& who's to say
it didn't die satisfied?
Driven in pursuit of all things bright,
a persistent, wretched ache
is rewarded
with relentless overabundance,
& I am picturing you wandering down
that grassy highway median
to be discovered by state troopers,
zombied off oxycontin,
in search of some such smoldering
release.
The blue fluorescence

brushes, almost imperceptibly,
a glare over these locked-up cars,
chained soda machine, abandoned puddle.
A light like a reluctant messiah
of limited evangelical radius:
one that attends, rescues nothing,
& yet provides some circumscribed
aspect of truth—
it shows some of what there is to see.
Pure access to the power source
would have sent the moth
embering to ground,
but to go bereft of light is to go
in search of purpose forever elsewhere,
baited by blood-urge
into the comforts of the night's
dumb, fleshy foliage.
Between us & the absolute,
the thinnest line—
we are lucky to have such borders
to beat our bodies against.
Brother, you tried to kidnap a salacious old man
& have him withdraw money from an ATM.
The drugs & criminality part & parcel
of an injurious world you claimed
as your own, so as not be its victim.
& we, your family, having circled incessantly
with judgment & expectations,
must adopt our own stances, perhaps afraid
to turn away & catch the shadow cast
by our own struggles, writ large.
In this dead lot I try to own
my own failures: to ameliorate,
to reach out, hear, advise.
I flicker with impossible past promises.
I write to you captive in a cell.

SHADOWMAN

Archipelag*OS

I grew up in
women. I grew
up surrounded
by women. I've
held & been
held by women.
I grew in their
shapes & was
loved by them.
I grew out of
their joys &
in the tribulations
put to them. I
surround my
self with women.
I fill my home
which is my space
with them. I imprint
with their stories.
I am imprinted
by them. I have
been in women
and women in
me. I have seen
myself a woman
in me. I have
watched them
die. I have bade
them eat, my
grandmother,
here, her very
favorite chicken
& dumplings

placed before her
at this roadside
restaurant off I-95.
She is laughing
heartily at
something I said
& so loud
that it's upsetting
the other customers,
her synthetic-looking
white hair alive,
light dancing
in her glasses,
the hole in her
now-still heart
whistling our
shared blood
a few more weeks yet,
having refused
the pacemaker.
She has me right
where she wants
me: alive.
We are exploding
uproarious islands,
this woman & I,
lost in tears,
the us of us
subsurface but
touching
in our sharing,
as my own heart
stumbles
into its now normal
arrhythmia.
I am for her
a dispelled
memory now:

lost acre,
or sprout
gone back
to field,
her figure
reconfigured
as if back
through navel
into our disappeared
generational
mother.
On the other
end of that
umbilicus,
I am fed,
peering
into the breach
of no real place,
already in
the history
of time
more shadow than man
in the shadows
of women.

ASPHODEL

Anth*OS

It's Lady's Night at the Second Circuit Court of Appeals. Lithe & lisping a longaniza-breathed "*Hey*, bitch," but sweetly sour, you arrive, love, paroled anew, descending stairs—du *hast mich, mein* champ—a fleet-footed Rocky feminista, fallen but resurrected, phoenixic as the crushed perfume of a booked botanical. Our lips clash like twin sisters. You slug a lager from the six-pack you requested I bring, then nimbly demonstrate, no punches pulled, a play performed "inside the clink": a "Society of Incarcerated Dilettanti" number—the ol' *stigmata'd-mouth-by-unforgiving-knuckles* exploitation show—invertebrating me with scenes of unshaven guards unlooping nightsticks, bulging to burst from the ugly amber of their lust. "Just *kidding*," you say, my Asphodel, always so inventive in your ways to street-sweep & re-gutter my trashy valences.

Six months in this time, & me single-living on the outskirts of a municipality of maybe, my heart an extrajudicial detention center for a wayward polyglot—baby, please, can we kibosh these insinuations of brickyard clit & cell-succumbed lipstick traces, or any mention of cult-flick scenarios involving former chemical addictions that remind me of times you'd upend my mental furniture, torch our family photos, or launch a speeding Vespa over the Warhol in Union Square? I get it; you paid dearly for approval. But cultivated urban rage is out, honey bear; dorkish opulence is the new Spanish fly. So let's re-immerse, see what's left to burn or bridge between us. Let's go get binary at the City Winery, maybe hit up Beauty Bar & revel in the whispery, watery earfuck of some electo-grrrl band's raw bandwidth, a hoppy vocalist who drops the bass like a velar plosive down our auditory canals, slithers a scintillating song of aural assonance along the chambers of your organ of Corti—& then later, consumed by whatever music hums between us, we'll caress to crescendo & thump each other's drums out. *Oh, my!* O my darkly grunt desire to have you in me. (Or hear me. My voice was always so comparatively minor—the saintly eruption of a tea bubble; a canary in a washer in your windstorm—whereas each note sent trembling along your vocal chords provokes my fault lines, flash floods my downtown, taps my shelled earth on a skillet.)

But I divest. Before your last arrest I tried hard to hinder your dealings; tried healing the abuser; tried to un-harken your brash hunger for other women, weapons on a mattress battlefield. It was always 5 AM with you, always a cold pillow molded in the pillowy shape of loss. Always a phone nearby in case you called, its blue light waking to my touch like some android antidote to your remoteness. I dreamt of car hoods heated beneath your hankering body, magnets pinning illicit pics to an imagined stranger's refrigerator. Understand, I'm human here—I can't just regenerate like an Originator. If you break it, you buy it... But I don't mean it. I mean: I need you, mostly, in pleasure's limpest instances, when you summon the wherewithal in me to want better things. I record those permutations in a blogography, citing love as a frail & tender fungus; collapsible as a fruit fly beaked by a fairy flycatcher, a feathered species listed as "Endangered, Least Concern."

But I do dream. Your face alive in my hands is a frigid body of water that eventually bloats whatever it cools, like television; that look crazing crevices through memories of my old life in the Spanish Legion, managing the orphanage, nights retiring before the corpulent cusp of Aunt Televisa's black broadcasting eye. I rivered a queen once for the win, Asphodel—do you remember how I won you? With a pout you'd bet a paper ring & frankly crooned, *I'll win that back one orgasm at a time.* But failed to say with whom. A crabswoman at the cleat, I dismissed your precious, petulant weather & dragged my pot in, catching your *fin* in my mesh. But you became a smaller, slicker animal. Virulent as language, mouth to foreign mouth you moved, indiscriminately, somehow satisfied to occupy the lowly status of *unresisting ingénue* to their myths (& misanthropy), enjoying perhaps the erotic infamy of becoming one of desire's devious allegories. Viral you entered me, too, in what I thought (ha!) was your weakest form. Until you slowly de-teethed my t-cells. Until you clotted my kidneys & caromed off my vascular walls like the hundredth margarita.

& here we are tonight, again, outside another courthouse, chatting like gadflies, arguing relapses, & me needing to say...I can't be with you any longer. & you recognizing weakness as I jungle-gym your knuckles with my nails, eye-bang your shallow ribs one melodious bar at a time. Netflix, the Marriage Act, my trip to Madagascar—nervous filler conversation. Sure, have another lager, Asphodel. Shirk the system. When you dance on the roof of my car, the court policemen feign displeasure. (Dance upon my tongue, I imagine, & feel flushed.) I could join you, but would rather erode with joy at having our bonds released again by sirens, & back to lock-up you'd go, a tragedy in renewable one-acts.

Our marriage was a simple crime, wasn't it? A misdemeanor brought before the hanging judge. Get in, get out, no traces left. No babies, no brooms; no cash exchange or credence; no reason, we thought, not to. A union devised in the moment; partly for a movement, maybe; for love & fun; & dissolved quite easily by barfly baronesses whose noxious perfumes one can't unwash from memory or bed sheets.

Clutching the bus ticket I bought—destination: your mother's house—you look hurt. How did you expect to find me? A liaison from our glorious past, devoid of seasons' reasoning? You were my wife, my republic, my butterfly Gemini. My spoiler of gardens, my gutshot, my greeny gritty window of sexual renaissance washed clean to worldly, drippy destitution. Goodbye, baby. *Baby*, goodbye.

& driving home now, the ugly barren storefronts frame the ultimate features of experience, Asphodel. The forget-me-nots erupting from the sidewalks haven't, Asphodel, forgotten. The moon hides its sister face for a reason, Asphodel. For fuck's sake, the Williamsburg Bridge has been overrun by a flashy hoard of teetering ectomorphic models & the chorus of their sultry exhalations delivers one name only, Asphodel. The mucked-up East River laps against your ruined shores & leaps upon the pylons, Asphodel, as condos on both sides peer across the gulf & blink in slow rotation like the frightful, needy inhabitants of bars. Asphodel, this streetlamp needs you! Of what importance would it serve without your loping shadow carousing about its spotlight like a mad conductor in a hurricane's eye, where insects manifest in the bulb's thought-bubble to fuck & die, fuck & die, their bodies the frantic text of some unreadable cosmic joke? Who will snub my missives, or kiss the sickle of my instep, or declare her wheaty pubic V my winter's harvest? Who else could break me into smile with a gauche pun involving the hardening rates & filler ratios of adhesives? Who but a carpentry foreman & total fop could reinvent the whole butch/bitch thing not as a trashy novel trope but as a life? & whose wild life stories (I of the boring lectures on public housing) could I possibly adopt so I might chatterbox & entice a tilted leggy fixture—somehow in four-inch heels, a sullen artsy Whitney type—into her boxy loft bed & black coffee in the predawn?

She wasn't terrible, but fuck, she wasn't you. This horrible fidelity to my infidel's lovely bits & bargaining chips, fall where they may—whatever we had, it was never dull.

Enough! Shit! My god, my mother's voice, a Space Coast heartache on a Harley, holding back my hair over the toilet as I regurgitate a Friday night's impressive combination of faux pas, my first foray into the liquidity of adulthood's less than enviable decisions. The deals you make & deal with. *Maybe next time you'll think twice before you try swallowing everything all up at once.* I'm building up my stamina,

Mom. I'm gonna be like you. I'm lobotomizing a drama geek, plucking out my baby teeth. I'm preparing for the roughneck world in which you floated unencumbered between campfire & filling station motel, between cocaine binges & the lucidity of a pay-per-day workforce's asymmetries. *Sweetheart*, she'd say, *you got a whole life yet.*

& yet. The sky has unbandaged its sunburned clouds too soon, Asphodel, & a pink scar threads the morning. The marine birds scatter like the white lies we tell ourselves. Bakery trucks in loading bays release the quicksand smell of bread & honey onto Metropolitan Ave, & I'd rather have you here again—among buildings that rise like uncredited actors, the strollers abandoned to empty parking lots, this sky too eager to impress—to leave you, again, at our home's steps. It's not that I don't want you with me. It's that to live, I need to learn to live without.

BEDFORD AVE L

Thanat*OS

This is the moment I tell you you will be okay
& this is the moment you say no.
I do not know who I am telling this to.
I do not know myself in this moment,
& I do not know you. But hey buddy, hold on.

This is the moment I tell you you will be okay
& this is the moment you say no.
I do not have the wherewithal to be present
& yet here I am, coaching you awake,
the violence in my head a clarifying bullhorn.

This is the moment I tell you you will be okay
& this is the moment you say no.
I find the train has taken your pants. Above you
the commuters press their rocking faces
to the elongated window, hoping for a glimpse.

This is the moment I tell you you will be okay
& this is the moment you say no.
The way it twisted you around, my wife said
she knew. But I do not know. Your purpling chin
abuts the silver car & I mumble, *I'm here, I'm here.*

This is the moment I tell you you will be okay
& this is the moment you say no.
Later, my brother, a fireman, to allay whatever
he saw in my expression, will tell me of watching a father—
doused in gas, his daughter nearby—strike the match.

This is the moment I tell you you will be okay
& this is the moment you say no.
You teach me what we are: a sad, sorry

human effort. Some barrier breaks & I feel full
of earth, conscious of what little separates us.

This is the moment I tell you you will be okay
& this is the moment you say no.
One second you're fighting another drunk straphanger,
the next saw you flipped onto the tracks. Forgive me
for being here, in this final, deeply personal space.

This is the moment I tell you you will be okay
& this is the moment you say no.
The other other man has escaped. I will later identify him
shivering in a lineup. The news will claim he's a murderer,
then flip: a schizophrenic you wanted to teach a lesson.

This is the moment I tell you you will be okay
& this is the moment you say no.
& you are right. The commuters, they run from us.
They run & are carried into a future no wider
than the pinched space between a train & its platform.

This is the moment I tell you you will be okay
& this is the moment you say no.
I do not know who I am telling this to.
I do not know myself in this moment,
& I don't know you yet—but c'mon, man, hold on.

II.

Death Economies

TOMORROW

*Avri*OS*

Today is not today, because it is still
yesterday. & yesterday was the day
before yesterday, & the day before that.
There will never be a new day so long
as we live in this, our long yesterday.
They did not take another black life
today, because this is no new day,
it's still yesterday, & the yesterday
we live in has been a long, long day.
People talk about tomorrow as if
they'd ever lived in a tomorrow,
but no one has lived in a tomorrow,
we just have today, which is not
today, but yesterday, & yesterday
we know has been a long, long day.
Many times a day I think about it,
this possibility of a tomorrow,
here in the heat of day, in what
feels like an irrepressible heat
of an interminable day. I think
about what it will take to turn
this day into something not this day,
what will bring the night upon us
& pull the heat from our bodies
& quiet us. Or I think of our bodies
quietly repairing in the night
between this day & whatever
comes after this day. I can sense
the new heat, & hope it is not
just a new yesterday. I can sense
it blending with the night until
there is no difference between
the two, until there is.

CHEERIOS

We're sharing stories
Tonight after maybe too many drinks
But among friends mostly
& with some good jokes behind us
We move into a new space
Of realness & the problems
Our world is facing,
& all the good communication
We are having in our lives
Making sure some miseducated others
Understand the ways they are *wrong, wrong, wrong*
& I am cornered by my own adamancy
& by the questions of a stranger
Into the telling of a story
& am soon relating (why? to complicate
This image of me, wine glass in hand?)
How my mother raised three kids
Alone on weekdays
On a hundred dollars a month
& refused food stamps
For as long as she could
Out of what I mistook as pride only,
Until one morning she collapsed weeping at the table
Over the last packet of dehydrated macaroni & cheese
& crumbs of Cheerios collected in the hip of a plastic bag
& admitted without words some final terrible loss
Before her stunned & unsure children,
& this guy suddenly beside me
Nods & says, "Whatever doesn't kill you—"

& I'm remembering this conversation
With more than a little guilt
On the corner of 76th & Lexington at 2 AM
Rousing a young, seemingly newly homeless woman
Out from under her hard stare
Over leveled kneecaps

As behind her the others sleep on, layered in thin blankets
& broke-backed corrugated cardboard
In this seven-degree night of perfect
Chill, this solid block of death,
& I'm offering her a sleeping bag
Which she will refuse
which she will refuse
& I will ask again, please,
it's only going to get worse,
& she will refuse
with a look I'll never forget
because it showed me who I was to her
in no uncertain terms,
ending with a final exhalation
that was a curse
on this the coldest night of our year

realizing why I grew so angry
so quickly
& turned upon this stranger
in the once friendly apartment, announcing
What doesn't kill you
kills you
   motherfucker
That you *is fucking dead*
motherfucker

knowing, yes, this isn't always true
but I in that moment
was already someone's child, again,
my fists on the table
watching this woman I love more than breathing—
her sobbing tenor stirring me to rage—
take a beating for me
as she collapses
into the unforgiveable arms
of another's service

ETHOS

"This piece, like myself, is a work in progress"

America,
          amore, I can't
I know
  survive you.

        Nor exist within you now without resistance.
        We can work to reconfigure & revive this bond,
        & rejoice! Or re-vivisect your callous joie de vivre,
        reviewing each vicious act captured on video.

I can't keep you—
  or keep you kept.

I can enclose you
closely   in mind
but not altogether clearly.

Americana, you are
a smattering of lush insults, a red slathering of lathe.

Please forgive my form.
I fit you
fitfully, & fearful
              & form myself
from our forced embrace.

I forget myself   in you
at times   at times

I confront you curious
for a cure of you.

There's a word I'd like to have.

By which I mean share.
By which I mean a word or two.

Originally I wanted nothing from you.
Then nothing but a wedding
        a weekend in your warmer climates
        a body full of bubbles.

              Brr went the bitter cold.
              Ping went the pipes.

Originally I was born & bred.
& read, to be an original
                  a burgeoning
aboriginal
           a bore
in short   appeased to be aborted
(if my ambition met no fruition)
           or merely applauded
for some hardscrabble, ramshackle work,
then weakened
       in the familiar ways
awaiting the final pause.

But in my *living*
I found in some others' lives a loving
generosity, folks gifted few grants
but giving in ways that held in contradiction
my own hoarded & squandered givens
so simply granted, & which I took for—
so into my pocket of imperfect selves I went
to rummage up better made goods
so I might best share in greater measure
some of my givens.

I researched & saw in my own scenario a seductive
& easily engageable amaurotic oversight:
a way to live with less personal contention, but

a life imaginable & available due in part
            to a social reflexivity & power afforded
by pale birthright & preconfigured anatomy—
            my bootstraps pre-constructed.

Hence (though I was raised poor as a putrefied palm tree)
myriad historical instruction
& social institutions
                    primed my more easy entry
into options.

So I began to watch more closely
what you were giving out   & up on.

'Murica, why is every dinner with you now
me staring at my fists?

But this is a breakdown scene, not a breakup.
A peace between us   is my preference.
Yet peace isn't the pleasant
settling into   we hear in the hopeful
& vaguely compassionate voices   is it—
it's learning to live
            on the shifting pinprick plateau
                        of a continental divide
formed from warring
elementals   struck together   & rising,
            with one side armed
            consciously or otherwise, intentionally or not,
with what they've been educated to suppress
in themselves & in others,
            an influence used to
            de-voice, deflect, contain.
& the other with ideas & bravery & bodies.

My new effort is self-
documentation in self-
reconstruction—

a humane voice
reprioritizing & re-identifying
while eking out its own place
in the scorched archive.

Think of this as my cumulative
directorial debut
                    the launch of an imperfect movie
                    detailing an imperfect movement,
beginning with this simple image:

        an updraft
        of snow
                    falling
        into orbit

& later obit.
        But not just yet.

I've brought you a pocket
full of pleases. A thank you.
A fuck you. A think tank.
A thunk trunk.

As I devise in myself in this short time
together   a systematic operation
                    of inclusion—
to catch all what I can that falls between
        & far outside
binaries.

To each the *having*
of their story.

These palpitations shocking your cities
might be mass transit
or mass exodus
                    my heart goes

out
to those with lives
on the lines

We have seen how
you treat certain stories differently:
between those charged
with protecting
            & those charged
on the spot

not minor clashes
but monumental miscarriages—

        & when again asked for your hand in marrying
the moment to the momentous
you always mumble *Maybe*...

& lose the color in your face.

I cannot complete the circle
of whatever vows—hand over heart—
I took by being born of you.

        We are, as children even, asked
to believe you are exceptional
        & precociously accumulative
                in your bettering—
        seeking forever the *more* perfect—
yet you're actually closer akin to
a messy confluence,
        a tornado of virtues & turpitude,
        a nation-wide compilation of life's
        vivid & fluid & interesting bits,
those examples of trans-
generational, trans-
national, lingual, gendered, trans-
spiring

circuitries of cohabitation & being
—work, health, wealth, yearn, earth, death—
from commerce to intercourse

& we can't buy benignly into any ameliorative myth
        when you move
from benevolent benefactor bright with generosity
to bewildering, brutish
        & unbearable
so quickly
            so often—

You were perhaps born
        of too simple
a belief system

by which I mean a terrible
(& terribly lucrative) belief
in your own inalienable rightness,
inconsistent with your gifts
& protection.

        Left unchecked,
this behavior
will sink
our sovereign selves
& run the streets dead red.

But I'm not here
pretending I might play
your machinating Ex
                or have you as my deus.

    I cannot
I know
accept you
except to accept
I am you   in whatever ways I am

33

& change
what I can about myself
      & what I can about you
to make you   a better *us*.

Like the lover
I am
I keep you
close.

But like the slow drift
of atmospheres
over city lights & fallow
                 fickle fields,
     I reproachfully
decline your borders.

WALL STREET CONFIDENTIAL

IP*OS

I gave up Nancy my wife for the private & inauspicious love of my pet komodo dragon. I gave up my vegan roots for Xanax, Goldman's, Ugandan beef. I traded Pabst Blue for Bluetooth, my nipple ring for a ranch in Naples. I learned everything has a price, especially people. I gave up people. That is, I gave up tangible currencies. I gave up the good cause & the fair fight. I gave up tax reform for insider tips, civic marches for skysurfing. I took escorts to the movies. I encouraged bootstraps, & still fry my own bologna. I once sold very, very high. I found Sensex not so Nifty so I fabricated futures data, pumped & dumped, hedged my bets. I huddled, negotiated, & undercut my mentors. Shorted LEH to a flat-lined EKG as ARMs exploded mortgages like RPGs. I missed the extra point, most of us did; wept & showered with the team. We agreed ours was a job for nobler men. Agreed it was a job for cannibals. We were ushered dripping through the corridors of public shame, pomp & spectacle, our bruises showcased, our greed paraded by pandering politicos we vacationed with. Dreamt of iron doors & Quantico. Instead, they refashioned us. With suits. The golden parachute of government. We were our parents' helioscopic shadows, precious & peripheral: a poorly inked Woodstock woodcut. The brutal game is back, with cutthroat algorithms. Hike the rate, rate the hike, hike the ball. Sometimes I still blush when folks ask for directions. Sometimes I still worry to think.

THE JOURNAL

*Whack*OS*

The Journal will be televised. The Journal was instrumental in lobbying Congress for a drabber but cleaner form of post-recreational love (Sugar-O-Not-Thy-Bowl-But-Bun-In-Oven-Salt Nondenominational Act of 2019). The Journal is how we knew the trypanites were never seriously substrata; how dinosaur bones were a ruse by our comic Creator—His beast implants; how the liturgical facts added up; how 'snowflake' could be worked into a limerick; & if brought before tribunal, methods to better sheath or blanch our oil-bloodied helmets. The Journal takes a southwesterly path causing rip-currents down through the Carolinas, or at least the one we've interviewed, a grand old dame from Lynchburg, tattoos of the heads of certain Supreme Court Justices rainbowing one scapula, & Reagan on the upper, inner thigh. The Journal is never unintentionally ambiguous. The Journal ups the ante on what we used to call "the news." The Journal hosts your favorite hate-speech dinner programming. In times of weakness, The Journal resorts to journalism. The Journal does not forgive. The Journal does not forget. The Journal recognizes the importance of separating out the "true lilies." The Journal accepts snapshots of gas cylinders, nano-armor, white nationalists, & rallying southern majorities in lieu of résumés, embraces eclipses as revelation, sleeps tucked into the south slope of the 18th hole at Trump Golf Links at Ferry Point. O to be naturalized in Scandinavia! To be a forgotten specimen no longer paid minimum wage to burrow into a right-wing think tank's terrifying convictions, with one's appetites free to explore the larger armoire of earthly delights! The Journal does not recognize earthly delights, denies having experienced a colorful genital shock & *coup de foudre* while standing stoically, sweatily before Matisse's *La Musique*, 1939. The Journal scrutinizes the scrutinizers, elephant-stomps the whistle blowers, empties not its pockets of loose change for beggars whose mouths have grown dangerously horizontal from methamphetamines. The Journal reconfigures voting districts to demarcate the "violent pockets" of your hometown. The Journal canceled its subscription to itself by robo-call. The Journal insists it jumped no shark, screwed no pooch, cheered against no Secretary of State Secretariat around the quarter bend of any final stretch. The Journal has witnessed the frozen screams of Pompeii & questioned the believability of their emotional responses. The Journal believes the crowd was larger than the other networks claimed. The Journal has created party informational tracts tasting of everlasting gobstoppers for children "with negative income." The Journal gives until it hurts (someone). The Journal, it should be noted, takes quite seriously matters of social decay & revolution. The Journal has extended the average length of a day but refuses to confide by how much. O but why not quit this job, go back to singing vocals for Savage Bear Lust, an American rock band formed in Greenpoint, Brooklyn in 2006, formerly Socks on Cocks, with a strong psychedelic slant that utilizes fuller sounds with live instruments that include a dyspeptic peacock & murderous accordions? Why sit at this computer typing in the diatribes of an employer known to tap phones, delete pictures of its enemies' pets, a Corp that has just bargained to turn state on the State for revealing state secrets? I must believe the Journal cares. Here's our toll-free number: 1-800-The-Journal-Really-Really-Cares. The Journal entered into the National Historic Registry of Right & Might in 1969. As if you really cared. If moral indignation is jealousy with a halo, as H. G. Wells suggested, the Journal is certainly not indignant, & another thing, you barely know the Journal, & yet you talk this way behind its back, lambasting those we seek to protect, as if you've never passed out drunk in a park with your junk out in the hot wet visible ether of July, or found your ignorance encyclopedic & blamed science in the attempted cover-up, with a host of old friends assassinating you with silence, the Empty Empire of Anomie striking back & the Great Cadillac of Kickbacks gone redly into the star-stung horizon. But fuck that—the Journal isn't hurt. Whatever. You are a harmless enigma made terrible by your own mad attempt at self-discovery. Let us help. The previous two sentences have been trademarked by the Journal. The Journal is responsible for the following release: "Oberon, a moon of Uranus, was discovered by "William" Herschel Walker during a third-quarter touchdown attempt, Vikings vs Dallas, in which he suffered a revelatory concussion." The Journal recognizes there is a disagreement as to the accuracy of this statement. The Journal understands, though, that history is a Hegelian argument, & boring if not engaged, especially at a rapid pace, 24/7, & besides, really, what's the point of plain-Jane truth if it fails to comfort or excite? The Journal does not incite or intercede; the Journal merely entices. The Journal has no regrets. Retractions are the refuge of flip-floppers struck by an over-zealous sense of responsibility to adhere to factual evidence. The Journal can almost hear them wheezing as they slip into the historical dark. The Journal records it, & posts its findings alongside images of a teen starlet whose sheer black dress reveals, look closely, a hint of slipped nipple. The Journal admonishes the starlet for her indecency for weeks, highlighting the various imbroglios of friends & family. The Journal hosts the interview of said starlet's tearful apology. The Journal hires her to take down other starlets. The Journal has its causes. The Journal helps excise the gun's report from gun reports, minorities from minority reports, the issues from the tissues. O to be a baseball great! Or an

Academy Award nominee! To think I could thank a fan for thanking me for being me! Instead I play Settlers of Catan in Java script & edit for TV. The Journal knows how hard it is. The Journal knows you try. The Journal expects nothing more. The Journal expects to find its pundits alarmed, its candy twizzled, its Oxford-educated personalities bumpkinified. The Journal is getting tired of being a lone voice in the wolf's wilderness. We can't go on. We must go online. The Journal alludes with the best of them, is a master of illusion. The Journal can name-drop with the worst of them. The Journal has read every book ever, so there. But the Journal is not here to step on you, it's here to lift you up! Encourage you! Console you. Without the Journal, where would you be? Who would you be? Who would you be being with? The Journal knows you. Come here; lay down. Prop up the legs. Let the Journal do the work. This is after all the Journal's job. The Journal is how you know you know what you know, & how you know you're right.

A BROTHER RETURNS

Omphal*OS

Maybe because I've had some minor
Heart surgery
& you're back in prison, & all the books
I send you
From Amazon keep getting returned
Because violence
Isn't tolerated, in literary form, at least, in the venerated
Penal system
Of the upper territories of Florida, but I've felt the need
To write not about loss
But losing, the incessant inescapable truth
Of our lives.
I've just read a story by Stephen King
Imitating Carver
& it's a pretty good story, & I think of all
The friends
Over the years who've shared with me their hatred
For genre & for books
In general, & I hate books & writers too, at times,
The whole Lineage,
The entire concept of the written word
& the accumulation
Of histories for self-glorification or entertainment
Or mere truth
Of evidence, the lie we tell ourselves of learning
From previous mistakes,
When you & I both know we learn best by living out
Regret in utter self-
Deflating repetition, dry-docking our hopes to pills
Or some other tangible
Replacement of the tangible. I wonder what the poor
Woman who woke
To find you bleeding on her couch, window smashed,

High on Oxy,
Thought you were there to do, & figure probably kill
Her dead.
Instead you wanted money to buy more drugs & be gone
From the horror
Of yourself, away from that person holding a woman's arm
As she dialed 911.
I wonder if you're glad she swung at you. I wonder
Why
You didn't bleed out in the parking lot of the hospital,
Or why you didn't
Just wait at her house for the cops to come pick you up.
I think it's because
You believed escape was possible; not that you'd beat
The rap,
Or disappear into a phantom car headed up I-95
Into the bluing morning,
Or be captured & let off by some errant mistake
Made by a rookie cop,
But that by trodding those miles bleeding in the dark
You'd find
Some aspect of yourself you'd been searching for
All along,
That suddenly, like the idea for a story, it would just
Occur.
I think we're each approaching some final project,
A place
To drop a stone. Not to mark out territory, but signal a center:
Here I stand.
I'd like to believe your project has something to do with grace & healing,
& redemption,
But I know it has more to do with grinding your faith into flour
& scraping some part of you
Off the fender of everyone you love & self-hating & forgiving your way
Into a place
Of relative comfort & peace of mind about the little time
You'll feel
You'll have left on the outside. & I'll be here hating

Myself in ways
I hope I can keep from you enough to share in some
Happiness
As brothers. Hoping you don't fuck up & go back
At age 42,
The age you will be when you get out, the age I am as I write this.
I hope our better wills
Break ourselves into something more living
Than mourned.
They say it will take three months for my heart to scar
Over & heal.
When I stand up to walk, I still feel the rhythm try to give way
& collapse me.

III.

The New Arts

THE POEM

*Top*OS*

*for {_ _}, & all his notions of what a poem might be, become,
become bankrupt by, catch as its second wind, or die as*

The one that writes itself. The decadent & self-consuming. The oratory. Every room. The alter of the pristine image. The altogether calm, placating voice of a ghost imparting its final secret in succinctly whispered stanzas. The rambling eccentric, phrases gone epileptic, a mind in its changing, a shiny bell, my parent's insufferable love & damning self-criticism, & fruit flies in September, which reminds me. The prognostication. The point maker. The moving center. The pained cry from a city's boiling vortex. The critical reinterpretation. The fawning philosophy, its homage begetting a neo- tag. The post-neo-upstart. The Googler. The ogler. The appetite suppressant. The bearer of dusky premonitions. The family breakdown as open-heart surgery. The implant. The shuddering in an outhouse of one's own creation. The lighthouse. The beaconless. The bright & beautiful museum maven on a stroll, O Jane, you crazy thing. Every room of text. The bon vivant, the bête noir, the bacchanalian adolescent immersed in undoing a century's aesthetic. The fractal forget-me-not. The fecal factoid. The hurt child. The chortling wan & wilting sympathizer. The synthesizing DJ of documentary. The downtown, uptown, mid-town rhapsody. The bucolic belle of balladry. The embarrassing aside. The heartbreakingly formal rant against The Establishment. The chatty freelancers' web of grumbling exquisite corpses. The hordes of stressed/unstressed syllables bench-pressing a strophe. Every room of text a honey. The unwritten poem. The pome. The Palme d'Or pantoum. The concrete architect. The bilingual love affair. The month I spent in Spain. This is not about you. This is totally about you. The list. The liaison. The laissez-faire. The mud under a hundred horses' hooves. The godless, the god-defying, the sufferer of God. The repetitive. The respondent. The rogue. This one time. This is how bad it got. Cheer up. Three cheers. Chernobyl. The bomb, which makes us always hereafter indivisible or invisible. The academic endemic, the cult of quietude, the asphyxiating b=(re:)a=t=h. This act of retribution, perhaps. Every room of text a honeymoon. This active contribution, perhaps. The retaliation against this, or its lack. The contrapuntal narrators as sparring partners vis-a-vis the brain's hemispheres. The galactic comic. The resurgence of once widely held beliefs fallen into ideological limbo. The flaccid cock. The inspired vulva. The coital romp, or "Erotics as a Breezy Dance Symposium in a Self-Correcting Ecosystem." The claptrap rap sheet photovoltaic photo shoot. The selfie. The popularity contest. The big prize. The flotilla of formlessness. The greenhouse diorama. The ecologically engaged. The swamp or bog pit innocent newly reborn as a naturalist receiving death. The urban youth vocalizing peril. The decay of decay. I just discovered this form yesterday. I just discovered my life has substance beyond me. Every room of text a honeymoon suit. My cat is sick again. My dog does not make sense. My spouse does not make sense. The eerie wandering eye-lust of the romantic. The doctrine. The divorce. Engaging this underlying current of dread. The re-emergent genius. The unreliably narrated. The fetishistic. The free fall. The elevated naturalism of the plastic garden foal. The translation. The transliteration. The fraud. The fraudulently hip. The hipster sincerely hungry for recognition of the pain underlying sarcasm. The hopeful. The angry medicated & their mothers. The apropos of nothing. The apoplectic apologist. Dear me. Dear John. Dearest, I don't know who I am anymore. Every room of text a honeymoon suite. The civil war. The rebellion against a repeat. The warnings of attrition. I as the infinite bass line. The lyrical id. The calculating enjambment. The operatic pornographer. The agitator. The playful emancipator of spatial echelons. Those distrustful of voice. The overlord. The ever-present. Dearest, my love for you exists in lists but listless wanders off to weird peripheries; will you learn to forgive my wandering ear? My strange confabulations, all in service of something beautiful & buckling to inch about your inchless waist, O ghostly no one, or ribbon about the delightful dancing hype I find hypnotic in its indifference to my deference? Every room of text a honeymoon suite with at least one love. Here's a blueberry, bitter as a Clinton. Here's a shipwreck, a glossary of current. Here's me beating time, & beating time. The last gun standing at high noon in a canyon of dust. The ode to the mite. Here's the fevered dream. The apocalyptic centerfold. The courageous. The war-torn. The shell, shocked. The kicked bucket. The lone cricket barking from a rusted Buick. The horribly alive. The abecedarian, the betrothed, the cancerous & debilitated. The enemy as sibling. The girl lost in a thicket of cymbals. The boy guarding a wicket of symbols. The song. The sci-fi phantasmagoric. The gory. The implausible epic of the Irish African King Gormund. The guilty. The final straw. The boycott. The eye obfuscated. The I, obliterated. My own trembling soprano. Every room of text a honeymoon suite with at least one lover. Here is my heavy heart in cursive, my huddled heart in print, my digital diaphragm going thump, scroll down, thump. Each camp a reenactment with a different lens. Each lens-maker focused on the slightest divergence. The grunted. The grotesque. The shout pitched just far enough to manage a meaningful exchange, or sadly too far for an audience of more than two. Voice like a light left on in an empty bathroom.

A hiss rising from the basement. The forgers & speculators. The open thefts of the desirous & demented. Image & idea. All so beautiful & bountiful. All a wonder. & here we are driving fast in a vehicle we can't trade in, with an expired license we can't renew. Nothing matters but that we reach the border, the wedding to be held there, these breathy nuptials. Brethren & sistren, gather together. Every one built with a word, my love. Every room of text a honeymoon suite with at least one lover left to wonder in it.

THE DANCE

*Khlor*OS: Score for a Modern Dance Entitled* Green

Impetuous Impetus

The crassly fashioned.
The crudely uttered.
The caped crusader as a crêpe crew saber. Consciousness
is interruption.
Even a hollow gesture informs.

Movement as text without shelf-life, with a poplife
provenance in kinetic pleasures, whose half-life is performing
whole notes of rote consistency & strength.

& joy.

There's always enough laughter to go around, so unlike gruel—
there's never enough gruel. Consider yourself.
Consider yourself at home. The kireji
of a haiku is a word representing the moment the poem
is cut, where consciousness is severed in its telling
& heralds a new thought: the wound as act of creation.
The closest English equivalent might be the caesura,
the drum thump of a middle pause, aid to memorization.
Then consider the non sequitur, which seeks
for its own sake, emblematic of movement in that it must cut
away or cut further into a thing
to continue, as any green-thumbed gardener will attest.

Fwomp, the dance instructs, meaning slow first, then whiplash-y.
Fwomp fwomp. The child in me claps &
stomps about, green as a comic Seuss egg, her magic handbag
a music & a means of perilous adventure & Atari possibility.

The Force & the Green Fuse

In certain circles, dance is a sport.
In certain circles, a deadly one. From certain angles.
For some, a circular sprint. Or sacrifice.
Like sand iguanas, the dancers breathe in green. What is green?
What is the "Green Agenda"? Apolitical as a popsicle,
which is hopelessly political, & parsimonious as a president seeking re-election,
it cannot be encapsulated by the entwined trunks of three miniature trees.
Or these translucent peacock feathers. This candle. This fuel.
The envious. The dollar. The decibel. A copper invested in rain's rattling change.
Jack Burton's lime-eyed noir-fried gal pals in *Big Trouble in Little China*.
Tatiana will go. Violetta will stay. Neither have a Green Card.
Sir Gawain & the Green Knight, Emerald Isle symbolism & vegetation
myths, where folklore is served green as a grunt.
As the unpronounced cherry. The next renewable.
The news, graphic as a gringo novella. Novel as a ginkgo gecko
focusing its filmy green eye. Incest plots are the new
young outlaw love. There, I said it. I feel your clean ruining
my green slate. Your tattoo-able taboos. The best part of green tea
are the dead leaves that nag one's sense of fate.
They lie & lie about & laze & laissez–faire our fears like unfazed lasers.
Don't worry, there's always enough new loss to go around,
enough competition to break our bodies like an oboe.

Lost, in a Sense; Found in Another

Dear deciduous dryad, I aim to process your private syrups,
would settle as a simple windowsill wildflower
a happy accident
opening its amino palominos to the bee's dripping knees.
I'd ravage you like horseradish, swell your tongue,
& curve the slick of each incisor. I miss you
like the moment misses a maker of moments.

You make me feel so Jungian.

Make me spring like sprung's a scrum.
The lung-like mint-scented split of your center
I favor, enter airy as a birch forest, bendy-flex
as my hung desire to have you slung about me.

Contrapuntal as celluloid & score
are core & stomach muscles gone wrong
but O so right, like the impetus to extinguish empire,
or another bee slathered in its own sweet scent.

Choice is paralyzing.
I ease into the act of watching you
become unobtainable. If I ease
too quickly, I obtain, but what I get is not you.
If I ease too slowly, you get elsewhere & I get nothing.
You move again, a bullet of brevity I'm anxious
to acquire, but acquire by acquiescing; & collapse.

The Offal & the Feral: a Fall

We go after the ineffable.
We go after what we see as inevitable.
We go after each other's throats.

The Ballet Russes enters the Grand-Guignol
& entertains. The body enters the world
a world & intertwines. Both capture flailing until death.

Go ask the wasp tail. Go ask the green leaf
why it balances the trembling dewdrop
on its kitten paw.
There's no bottom to our greed for life.

Too much, though, & we grow bored.
Care little. Offer less.
Bathos a kind of tragic
fulfillment.

Watch how we break this world right quick.

O Helios, you power the leaf's circulation
but cannot stem the murderous algal upchuck of an ocean bloom.
The leatherback sea turtle fills a shallow pit
with ping-pong-ball-shaped eggs & when they hatch the maritime birds
will gorge themselves to gluttony; come night the survivors
paddle sand toward the light of either moon or highway lamp.
Are you going my way? Have we gone? The new Pacific
landmass is constructed entirely of plastic—
mountains of dew, forests of Sprites—
the condition of mankind reflected
in a hundred trillion plankton nuclei.
It is a perfect metaphor for itself—
green as the day is long,
deep as our willingness to forget it.

Unscrolling, as a Principle of Pleasure

These aren't, in one respect, the first
dancers to do this. The opposite is also true.

You work at play until you're tired.
My memory breads into instances,
renditions of us in this position—
how the body fits into wedges,
tucks into itself at energizing angles.

The tense blue vein wrapped about an engaged Achilles
is what I know of love. Muscle memory is a mechanical constable,
rigid constraints snapping body
to form, hi-ho. Hum. Sometimes we blow a gasket.
Sometimes a gymnast. Our muscles, by definition, define us.
Memory is muscular. A stronger one I keep is of the soles
of her feet, a crenulated shoreline. Her voice terse
as a clothesline, as she faces away.

The corrugated heat sleeve on my coffee cup
is patent pending. One day movement

will be made proprietary—imagine these breaths
expirated in intriguing couplets as a buy one, get one free.
Imagine the new market of lovemaking.
The bear & the bull. The vertical & horizontal markets.
The way cloth hangs from a body
can add or detract from presence. Divide orgasm
from organism & what you get
is a different way in. Getting out is easier. It seems the world's job
was to invent people so nature could peer back at itself.
& then help everyone stop breathing.

I envy the immediacy of her art—
how one seemingly natural gesture erases its past.
The body in terpsichorean movement erases the viewer.
She closes a fist & I'm gone.

Postscript

Dance is the apparatus of body
in ecstatic curiosity.

The emphatic spin-cycle of desire
& a release like resurrection, or reintegration.
No one is a totality, & none are autonomous.

At the end we are left with nothing
& more.

THE FILM

*Eg*OS*

The film you just watched tells two parallel stories: a struggling musician who also happens to be the pastor of a Congregational church is forced, ordered really, to choose between (A) joining Cannonball Adderley's Quintet in 1965, via a time-traveling gazebo, but only after helping Benny Motte print & distribute copies of Swift's then possibly treasonous *Gulliver's Travels* (I'll just assume I don't have to explain the conspiratorial connections), between that & (B) halting a hoard of rebels dead-set on destroying the Kurpsai Dam's hydroelectric power station in the modern era.

The second, take a seat—no the other chair—confirms certain suspicions I've had about art as a reliable means of ultimate change. That ding means we have to change chairs. Yes, get up.

As I was saying, the shooting gallery is a rather complex metaphor, especially in one's understanding of the detached observer, such as the ethics constituting a photojournalist's respect for his own uninvolved, & therefore ultimately unbiased, approach to atrocity, as not witness but documenter. The Sudanese child & the vulture, for example. The Bang-Bang Club?

There it is again. Whichever chair you like. It is obvious now that the national obesity level has reached unsustainable proportions; unsustainable in terms of the actual household incomes necessary to maintain individual healthcare costs. These aren't my figures. But I really find the charts a bit scary, don't you? In the very least disheartening. Check out this one. Just insane. No, take this one across from me. Have you ever heard of distraction psychology? Of course not, I just made it up. A-1 bullshit detector you got there, I can tell. Just need to verify you're on board. We value your insights, & truth is the great negotiator. I made that up, too. Yep. There's no real pattern or sequence. You comfortable? Great. People find this next part stings a bit. Or tickles, depending. Here, let me just spread these out.

Okay, as you can see...let's try to get through this without much fuss, okay? Nobody is passing judgment. These are for informational purposes only, & will be destroyed. All part of the process. As you can see, this is you parking in the hotel lot. & this, the camera in the bathroom. The bedroom. The laptop. Enter the cuckoldrix. Is that a word? The exchange. The act, or deed. The deed. The act. But, look here. The website. The hits. Quite popular. You were young. The internet, right? Never forgives, never forgets. Every Senator that comes from our children's generation will have a video too, don't worry.

Slide over. Let's face the screen. This thing, this toggles back & forth, like so. When the images appear you turn it this way to measure how bad it makes you feel; this way if it makes you feel good. It's less about accuracy than a vibe thing. My words may or may not coincide with what you see. Okay? Let's begin.

Dirigible. Pharmacy. Mudslide. Macroeconomics. Antwerp. Mouthsex. It is a word. Yes. If you can Google it, it's a word. Let's continue. Simpatico. Allegiance. Marketing. Freedom. Interpretation. Standards. Illegals. Nazis. Detroit. Liberal. Endgame. Prophecies. Foxes. Amendment. Loyalty. Succession. Very good. It's nothing, really. A study in polysyllabics. Ding! It becomes a sort of background noise, doesn't it? I'll come to you.

What if I were to tell you the entire time we've been in this room, we've been pumping in a carcinogenic air-freshener. The lemon-y smell, yes. Would you believe me? Okay. How would you describe the smell. A: waxy. B: medicinal. C: fruity. D: chemical-ly. Now, you are more inclined, you think, or less inclined to believe me because I'm wearing a lab coat? Interesting. We're not really, you know. Yes, the chair in the corner, please. Just walk over. Walk normally. Focus on where the walls meet.

Now whatever you hear, I don't want you to turn around. Just stare straight forward & focus. We ready? Okay, here goes.

I am your son. I have been searching for you for thirteen very long years. Uh-uh, no...forward. You abandoned me at a fire station in Port St. John, Florida, after the.... I grew up thinking you were dead, too. Random car accident. What they tell children. I grew up in a trailer, actually. My family was, um, fucked up, you could say. But I was lucky, they focused their anger more at each other than at me. I was good at baseball. Bad at making friends. Um, decided against college. Worked at Gannett News Service stacking *USA Todays* onto pallets for the night shift. I'm not going to tell you how I found out about you, because I would be endangering a person who is very dear to me. I respect that person. She was a friend, a teller at a bank. A national bank. That day, shit, I looked you up & there you were. Two kids, remarried. Same coast. Thought that was interesting. Two years on the job & a drunk forklift operator drops a stack of pallets on my legs. Please disregard the bings, dings, what the fuck ever, I need you to sit still & listen. My leg had to be put back together, reconstructed, so I had some time on my hands. I followed you. Online. Later in person. I lost a girlfriend once, when I brought her along &

54

showed her what I was doing. You may not remember, but I taught Julie how to hold a bat. On the playground. This was like…seven years ago. She seemed like a happy kid. I would have liked to have had a kid sister, I think. I let her keep the bat, maybe you remember? Yellow, it wasn't hard, it was plastic. I know children. Anyhow. I couldn't go back to work, couldn't stock, couldn't wait tables. It's hard to move. No, I mean physically. Move, not move on. If you noticed, I sort of just slid from chair to chair. I have trouble walking now. Okay. So when I landed this job like six months ago, they said I'd be traveling. But my legs, right? Well it turns out I fill a quota. Yep. I'm actually in demand. Very much so. & when I found out they were showing the film here, in this mall, in this town, well…& your name on the focus group list, are you kidding me? For real?

Ignore it. No, ignore the fucking bing. Seriously. Please. No, please! I know it's irritating. I'm here all day. This is my job.

Here, take this notepad. Here's a pen. I want you to draw whatever animal comes to mind. It doesn't matter if you don't think you can draw, everybody can draw, it's just that some people draw better than others. I'll wait. I've got all day. This is what I do. Continue.

Hey that's not half bad. You should give yourself more credit. I'll just take that. There is, however, one thing I need to tell you. One thing that's been on my mind. I just wanted you to know, well, that I forgive you. Thank you for not asking for what. Thank you. I just might need you to sit there & let the word sink in. Okay? Okay.

Okay, you can turn around now. Here, there you go. Now, now, there we are. Just keep the whole box, we have plenty.

Ha ha, ding!

Okay, firstly, are we okay? Okay, so then, truthful answers: how close was I with the details of this part of your life, to your memory & knowledge, one to ten, ten being extremely accurate? Just the details able to be verified by you. Excellent. Okay, secondly, how close was I in my imitation of your father's voice? As you remember it. Good.

Well, we thank you very much for your participation. That coupon's good in any of our retail outlets. No. No. I really have no idea. All of the information we have is publicly available, if you know where to look or who to buy it from. No, most of it is stuff people generally give up for free, posted online in one place or another. Yes, snails are quite common. Mice, roaches, lots of vermin, outdoor bugs…things of that nature. We had one person draw an eagle. Yes, just follow this hall, hang a left at the end, & you'll bump right into the exit interviewer's office. She's a licensed psychologist, so all of your questions, she's your gal. She has the copy of the contract you signed. Oh, & the, what did you choose? The inspirational poetry calendar? She'll have that, too. Again, thanks so much. Your participation has helped us tremendously. Tremendously. Take care.

What? Yes. I'm ready. Ready ready. Wait, let me set out the folder. Okay okay. Cue bing. I will never forgive any of you. I could live to be a hundred &...

Hello! Welcome! Jon is it? Can I call you Jon? How did you enjoy the film? Fun stuff, huh? Well for me, here, sit here in this chair, the film as I understand it tells two parallel stories. Feel free to interrupt me with any questions. Feel free.[1]

---

[1] Letters struck from the working script of the play *The Film* are evidenced in gray lettering, said to be used "for purposes unknown" by the director of the film version of *The Film*.

Brief Interviews with the Crew of *The Film*
for the Special Feature Anti-Cinéma-Vérité Documentary
The Filming of The Film, Directed by David "Moue" Oliet

TIME	VIDEO	AUDIO
01:00:01	Director	Film is a struggling music: to be the pastor of a rational force or a cannonball's traveling gaze? A set destroys the modern second— a sea, the air confirms. Art be hanged, we change. The gallery is a metaphor of the observer. Ethics constituting a photo, involved & biased, document examples. It is obvious now that the national eye is unsustainable.
01:00:23	Producer	The actual house is necessary to maintain individual costs. Figures I find scary, disheartening, just insane—

01:00:32	Composer	Take one across a yard of traction.
01:00:36	Actor	Psychology—or made-up bullshit—can verify you're on board.
01:00:43	VFX Crew	We value your insights.
01:00:46	Screenwriter	Truth is the great negator. I made that up.
01:00:52	DP	There's no real… pattern or sequence. Comfort stings or tickles, depending. Try this: judgments are information. Purpose will be destroyed. Part of the process, as you can see, is you. The camera is the exchange.
01:01:09	Whiskey	Look here.
01:01:11	Critic #2	The popular you young never forget. Every generation will face the screen. When the images appear, you measure how it makes you feel. This way it makes you.

58

01:01:22	Senior FX	It's less accuracy than vibe.
01:01:25	Script Rx	Words may or may not coincide with with what you see.
01:01:32	PA	Pharmacoeconomics. Let's continue.
01:01:36	Editor	Simpatico.
01:01:39	Foley	Allegiance.
01:01:42	Marketing	Marketing.
01:01:45	Director	Freedom.
01:01:48	Actor	Interpretation.
01:01:51	PS Mixer	Standards.
01:01:54	Props Master	Gazelle. Game props. Foxes.
01:02:00	Costume Designer	Loyalty.
01:02:03	Stunt Person	Success.
01:02:07	Script	I become a sort of background noise.

01:02:12	Camera	What if I were you in this room?
01:02:18	Craft Services	Cariogenic, fresh lemons.
01:02:22	Tag Line	Believe.
01:02:31	Blogger: Director:	How would you describe them? Wax fruit.
01:02:38	Insurance	I am inclined to invest in knowns.
01:02:45	Extra/ Background Actor	Walk. Walk normal. Focus. Turn around. Stare forward. Focus.
01:02:53	Gaffer	Ready? Okay. Arc!

01:03:02	Book Author	For years you abandoned me
		    (a station?)
		      Saint John.
		    I grew up a random accident.
		    I grew up really fucked up.
		I was lucky.
		      Focused anger
		is a friend. I worked
		at stacking days onto nights.
		
		    I'm going to tell you
		    how I found out
		    I would be a person
		    I respect:
		    Saint Bank-that-shit.

01:03:28	Trailer	Look here:
		    Two kids married
		      a cat.
		That's interesting.

01:03:33	D. e. machina	A drunk forklift operator
		         drops a sack
		           of pale pigs—
		the villain
		follows a girlfriend
		to the grave.

01:03:45	Best Boy	(She seemed like a happy kid.)
01:03:49	Key Grip	I wave like a kisser in heat.
01:03:52	Armorer	I war like any good table: hard to move, physically. Move. I have trouble walking now.

01:04:00	Sound Design	What moths
		    traveling
		    but my legs?)
		
		     I quote Lynch:
		Film is fifty percent sound.
		
		Everybody draws.
		Some draw with what is there,
		some with what is missing.

01:04:13	Moviegoer	Just keep the box plentiful.
01:04:18	Editor	Answer— how close was I with the details of this part of your memory?
01:04:25	Director	Knowledge: One extremely accurate detail able to be verified by imitation.
01:04:32	Cigarettes	Father's voice.
01:04:35	Online Piracy	We hanker for your participation.
01:04:40	Moonlight	Hat-upon-God.
01:04:43	Award Show	A fortune of public vail.
01:04:48	Drug Dealer	If you know where to look, who to buy it from.
01:04:57	Patience	It is stuff people generally give up for free.

01:05:03	Prod. Designer	One place or another. Sails are quite common. Caches of vermouth.

01:05:13	Director	Nature wages just this:
		at the end
		              you bump
		right into the Exit.
		
		Never offend psychology.
		Question your gut.
		Why choose inspiration
		              over hard work?
		
		You will never
		forgive yourself
		              for shit.
		
		Film
		is interruption.

THE SCORE

Ech*OS: Lyrics in divergent entropy

I. by Operation Ivy[a*]

Tucked into a fallacy, / fucked to hell by alchemy,
led drugged to dribble helplessly on economy's trace chain.
Revolutionized totality / is televised reality
as we squander sympathy and simply settle scores.

II. by The Magnetic Fields[b†]

The platypus is polyphonic.
The Serengeti is serene.
Creature Features teach us fear of bleachers
            and disease, screeching meteors, mutants, madmen, and each other,
as Baudelaire, ham-hearted flâneur, lectures preachers on the spleen.

III. by Tom Waits[c‡]

Got a bottleneck of hooch, goin' downtown. Got a
Farrow-lookin' smooch, gonna' make the rounds. Got a
finger with a blister, a meal-mouthed Uncle Fester,
a contrarian Stradivarius that lingers like a dreamer.
Pork chops, lamb chops, front-row seats. A diner
of maligners singing buffalo feats. A shotgun wedding
and out the bars begin to roll/ a smattering of cretins
aint worth the mud up off the flo'. Got a high-stakes
headache with a lowball blues. Got a girl named Mable
wearing hand-me-down shoes. Got a gun without a
barrel, like a Cain without an Abel, and here's a two-bit john
in moccasins dealin' queens under the table. Fan fare,
March Hare, Indian night. Twin sisters cinched in
hula skirts that graveyard-shift as ties. A healer
in kimono reads tea leaves for all the tourists / and
all around the docks you hear the windfall of the purists.
Got a bottleneck of hooch, goin' downtown. Got a
chicken that won't roost, gonna' make the rounds. Got a
man on the accordion / says he'll get me born again
but I stole Satchmo's tattered soul and wear it fast and loose.

'Milton's Antihero[§]

Tucked into a fall, fed by a
rugged rib.   Bless my chain.
Revolt: a levied
wander's path and simple sores.

[†]Health Scare at Mount Sinai Medical[¶]

Help us, polyp.
(The engine
rears.) Teach us fear,
ease. Re-chime rants, mad and other.
A bare-hearted lecture spears the seen.

[‡]Brooklyn Noir (What Dick Saw)[‖]

Go tattle, go down—go
arrow go rounds. Go
finger a mouth, clef
a contra, rat a divider,
pop a cop, front a diner,
align a shotgun, wed
at bars, roll a sting, *fin*
a worm, off the high-stakes
head, cow a blues gal, name a
ring, shoe a gun, hut a
bar, lie in a blue john
in Queens, under-tab a fare,
march twin sisters, cinch
a skirt, graveyard a healer,
kimono a TeeVee tourist,
run the docks, heart a flirt,
bottle hooch, downtown a
chick, make the rounds, go
on the 'cord, get born again—
bet a soul and lose.

[Five and Seven said nothing, but looked at Two.
Two began, in a low voice, "Why the fact is, you see,
Miss, this here ought to have been a red *rose-tree,*
and we put a white one in by mistake..."]

§

Tint of red, bless my revolt.

¶

Hears a chime, hearted.

‖

World is as the Queen's red rose.

a.

Unfortunately, chemical engineering makes us sick.
A bad economy beat Gregory and the basilica.
The *actual* production revolution.
These problems can be expected.

b.

Duck bills on the Serengeti Plains. We know that fear is amaretto.
Meteors, disease, madness, and then...*click*.
Tina thought Robert was blue-green. We heard this is very important.

c.

So, to Wayne's Wine Company. Even
now: a born leader, a Capricorn.
Finger balloons, cooking, fishing, his uncle
Stradivari and tender love.
In particular, with a good pig. The South is
rock bass swimming over cherry blossom.
A marriage that was forced,
his first, for little reason.
This is not flower dust. This is the biggest risk.
Bruce has a stingy disease. I may be a girl,
but I'm not his old shoes. I am a weapon without a permit,
the NATO administration and the ACC, with two free
hooves, a queen of the fan,
India's lunar night rabbit. The brothers Arrufat
provide estimates of spare parts, as well as fires at night.
Spermatophytes, tea travel, and clothing.
I live listening at the door of fundamentalists.
So, to Wayne's Wine Company,
to contact the hole within.
"Harmonics are born," he said.
Flight and motion in space and Armstrong and deadly fast.

THE PERFORMANCE

*Kud*OS*

1   Narrative is dead, she thought, then wrote it out.
    & yet each collision of unlike words evoked an imagined history & reasoning
    of their pairing, she thought, which kept each reader reading differently.
    'Amphibian gun lust' & 'anthropomorphic argyle.'
    She put her pencil down & stared at the letters. Patience was part
    of the performance, a way into process, which she valued utmost.
    She could feel the audience's anticipation bristling in the darkness
    of the auditorium beyond the lights. Behind her, a large screen broadcast
    her hands on the page. She picked up the pencil.

10   'Indiscreet, unutterable orchid lug nut.' Then crossed it out.
    'Intrepid aphid actuary.' Then crossed it out.
    Then she wrote 'old man' & instinctively cringed. What hope
    was there in such a well-documented relationship between these words?
    Where the music? The sonic click? Where the shifting consciousness?
    Someone coughed. She crossed it out.
    But there it was again, & she went to write it again, but it had already changed.
    'Old door.' She lifted her head & spoke it. & found a new word
    in the saying. 'Older,' she wrote, noting the easy power of reflexivity.
    'Older doorman.' 'Alderman,' & then: 'alderman dementia.'

20   The light encircling overhead was a trap. & her father's face was the darkness
    of what lay beyond herself in the auditorium & in these words,
    which changed within her without any urging or provocation she felt privy to.
    'Elder otherness' & 'dimensions.' 'Airy overlord' & 'demonstrably.'
    How time & language & power curlicue into each other, demonstrating...what?
    She felt them out there, slipping into their own specialized inferences.
    'Any airy overlord is elder otherness of demonstrable dimension.'
    She crossed it out. Then patiently rewrote it. Did it hold some truth yet?
    'I ape the emptying of otherness.' Seizing upon this, her internal editors:
    Seizing on this, her internal editors: *Locate & trouble all easy assumptions.*

30   *Address barriers, blind spots. Whose words, which power, what service, context?*
    Am I playing? Am I instructing, plotting, pushing, parroting?
    Another cough from the audience.

As part of the performance, the audience was asked to live-tweet the event;
tweets that later appeared on-screen were rendered anonymous.

Audience Twitter Feed: #ACPerformance or @anitanewme

1   This place is a dungeon smells like feet
      Refreshments of some kind would bring in more people. Just sayin.
      Love the new bangs Porf Anita! So exciting!!!
      Dr. Marissa Anita performing @ArtsCenter. Surefire titillation.
      i am a dustball on a condom on the bloated cock of america
      8/10 would do
      My favorite teacher is about to #performance
      Expect the unexpected -Gandalf
      Nobody is talking about Syria #genocide
10   dafuq?
      I saw Amphibian Gun Lust play the HelterSkelterDome in '13.
      Gun lust.
      She should be a hand model
      Good idea to go with the written version of John Cage's 4:33. Nope.
      I love the big screen! Her hands ahve so many cracks in them.
      Already have like 20 ideas for my thesis!
      Today in the jungles of Higher Ed we spy the irritated cattywampus.
      Nothing remains anonymous.
      How many students I wonder consider the pencil a device of antiquity?
20   I am Jack's twitching eyelid of boredom.
      Boulder. Border. Folding. Smolder.
      Performance art should be a performance, no?
      Hell is a mandatory performance for art class. #FML
      Turn down the heat in here please!
      People are paying her for this. #needadrink
      Not as dope as seeing Yoko at Strawberry Fields NYC but sooo #inspirational
      Is this supposed to be poetry? #yawp
      finally real art at the arts center
      'An overlord of elder otherness.' #describeyourdadinfivewords
30   Language is the real performer. The political act of utterance.
      Why did she feel the need to make herself so big? #thinkaboutit
      Doing close to nothing is hard because it demands all of you. #Abramovic

'I the otherness of empty ego.' Then:

'I the alderman of reason's conspiracy to outwit itself through language.'
She crossed it out & set the pencil down. Behind & above, her enormous hands
glowed on the enormous screen, apart from her & yet her representation,
digitized, faded, alien, almost tragic, possessed of an unnatural spirit,
fleshy but thin, cracked, insect-like, quasi-religious, as if each held gesture
were a station of the cross, captivating, boxed-in, captive but looming.

40   'Gun gone arachnid,' she wrote, but the time for this sort of music had passed.
Where was she? From the outer dark came that familiar sound
of members of the audience testing their seats.
She noticed, at the very edge of one thumb, the raw beginnings of a hangnail
& picked at it. Someone gasped. She turned to see her blood on the screen.
She felt this was her first real failure, but pushed herself to continue
or the next twenty minutes would be grueling.
She wrote, 'As one who is reluctant to separate image creation from intonation.'
Then: 'As one who imagines one intoning creation, imagines the breath arriving
before the word, one must also recognize image arrives before understanding.'

50   The gallery produced a few smug responses, pleased with themselves.
She admired her skin creases for a long time, wanting to strike through them.
Was this how it would go? With dialectics & divorces?
Meaning found only in the opposition of ideas
& structured binaries? Was sound alone capable of providing such rigorous
a pleasure or profound an understanding?
'Bird.' Then: 'Bird.'
She wrote the word out until the letters lost their shapes & bloated cursively.
She followed through them one uninterrupted line.
She wrote: 'Ritual celebrates conclusions.'

60   She wrote: 'Clap for me,' & waited. Several nervous claps sprang up.
She wrote: 'Make a cow sound,' & there came several moos.
To her left was a small screen she was reading. For a moment she was very still.
She wrote 'How many of you would like to see me undress?'
Silence. A chuckle. 'I will walk slowly around this desk. I will carefully take off
each item of clothing, letting them fall to the floor in front of me.
I will hop up on the desk & recline, and slowly spread my legs.'
There came whispers.
'I will pull my panties aside' then crossed out panties. Wrote 'underwear.'
Crossed it out & rewrote 'panties,' slowly, with mild provocation.

70   'And slowly slide this pencil as far as it will go up into my uterus.'

I write on projectors for a living #YOLO
somewhere between blah and meh #anitabreak
Pencil and screen as conduits #thethinresistancethatisart
Paper means fragility and impermanence. At what cost?
fuck macs apple is destroying china
"Otherness of empty ego" is an empty phrase.
Fuck China #MAGA
40   Reason's conspiracy? Maybe you should teach in Kansas #evolution
I like how she pauses to think. More people should do this.
The shift from agent of performance to provocateur was seamless.
Ze plot thickens
My butt fell asleep. My brain is jealous.
My baby is kicking! You are wonderful Ms Anita!
BLOODY FINGER WTF!!!
Grotesque gigantic hangnail picking was grotesque.
I wish they were streaming the comments behind her, they are hilarious.
I just threw up a little in my mouth.
50   Blind people will enjoy this in a different manner.
Did you just give a shout-out to Jesus?
Is the point to ignore you and read the tweets? Because if so, good job.
Blue phone lights bunker/ down in the hot theater/ glowworm pandemic
I'd get up in this bitch.
Best thing ever but I'm biased.
420 4eva
Bird
Bird.
bird
60   JD you asshole I hope you get expelled for writing that.
i knew it this is about #ritual
Clapperaperdingong
Mooooooooooo! We the herd! Obey sheeple!
TIL that people are disrespectful fucks.
This whole thing is about jumping the gun on conclusions beforehand
OH SHIT! WTF! Wild ass teacher getting naked!
Art equals nudity and shock-factor nowadays. Sad.
(0)(0) show them to meez
The body is a temple, folks.
70   You have my attention.

Giggles. A hushed *nah-ah!* The sound of two, perhaps three auditorium chairs
slapping against their backs.
The shuffling of legs & purses drawn aside for passersby.
'Clap for them,' she wrote, & now the claps came louder,
harried by hoots.
'Who are these people?' & the calls came louder still.
'Who are we and what do we want?' she wrote as fast as she could.
'Tell me what you want! Shout it!'
It took a moment, but then someone yelled an answer. Another joined.
80   Soon many more members of the audience were obliging.
A chorus, she thought. It empowers as it risks. Until it risks nothing,
haven been empowered. She listened as the tensions fed each other.
When she could no longer distinguish between voices, she scribbled:
'You need no longer be yourself or be a self restrained' & set them free.
The screen behind her blanked, then read: '@anitanewme I like being in
            third grade again, this is fun. Will we be making noodle art?'
Then: 'OMG this is a shit storm @anitanewme.' Then: 'Viva la revolution!'
Each message was addressed to her. A person. A placeholder.
WHERE IS YOUR GOD NOW! '
'Preach ;)'
90   'Everything I write goes on the big screen because I will it.'
'I get u. Nobody else do but I get u.'
'I absolve myself in you.'
'Great job Professor Anita!'
'#Fuckdapolice!'
'I'm just going to leave this here 8===[) - - -'
'Bravo.'
'Um...should someone call the cops?'
'It was a pleasure to be part of this.'
'SSSSlut BBBBomb'
100   'She's on Twitter now that's why she's typing tag her to show up! Testing 123'
'Entomos. The dissected sections, dissected."
'loco perra'
'A soul is not an accompaniment, antithesis of, it is the very center'
'Soul as construct.'
'Tits or GTFO'
'Pencil you promised.'
'This is THE most amazing thing.'

72

Your frustration deepens my joy. It's perverse. Your inaction revives.
I was feeling pretty connect but you blew it.
Underpanties.
wut?
Is it uterus or vajayjay? I guess the whole thing is technically the uterus
I will clap for you because I am your donkey boy.
We embolden each other's reactiveness, and that reactiveness divides us.
Off the hook in here!!!11!1
And there go the Republicans...
80   Prudes exit stage left.
Imagine intimacy as subscription service. #postporncamming
This building is owned by the university we should not be wasting funds
         on things like this. This is a mispropriation of funding.
Oh fuck off and get lit! This is awesome.
We transit in lonely multitude. We emit a curious note.
Doors opened in rapid succession by a sudden and seemingly permissive wind.
We respond to respond. Do you wait for permission? Who is your authority?
Inhabiting space is a privilege afforded by bodily and material power.
Inhabiting voice a value: even if artifice/avatar/imperious/anonymous
Inhabiting the imperfect, I hit refresh for dictation. Amalgamate to express.
90   A soul is an accompaniment. Since it does not exist naturally, we must build one.
A self is a series of substitutions, striations.
A spirit is a seal, keeping desire from satiation. One destroys the other.
The body is a sampled state in semi-awareness. I use it to get by.
The erotic is a hypnoidal state. I use it to disedify.
The word is statute. I use it to touch, warp, dispel, mythologize, prompt, subvert
How about you? I use it to weaken, love, harken, help, hurt, harass...
How about you? I'd like. to work. though this. with you. personally. no joke.
I'd like to build in me a means to better accommodate your voice. No pressure.
I'd like your invitation to do so. No hazard. Not a test. Look here:
100   I'm making you a story to depart from. Or into. Or defend. Or destroy me with.
Is it easier if you imagine me faceless, a self-conducting algorithm of potentiality?
Is this the new sex? Am I a star? An advert? A character? A conviction?
Is pithiness a gateway to your trust? Will you have me? Where do trusts join?
Is my offer to please, a soul's salesmanship, worthy of Followers? Likes? Loves?
Is there a we we can agree is us? Is this sempiternal? Have you left? You miss me?
What of myself remains in hashtag? In this place of shame and shamans.
Is love for me here a spatial love? Are you reading me into existence?

'Constraint opens the imagination's borders. Not a weakness.'
'#freestyleacademia'

110 'I am a sextpert.'
'Wasn't this supposed to be about what exactly?'

We break the language with our shattered histories. We'll rebuild. Unify as Vox.
Words are a poor pledge. A proximity. An intimation, not summation.
110   Utterance is an attempt to return, revive, regenerate. Reverse abortions.
This construct gives consent. It lays down. I insert this voice into its uterus.
          All of you into my uterus.

IV.

Internal States of the Garden Thrush

QUASIMODOS

This garden thrush.
& that one. & this one
over here. Mates, matte-
mediumed & collaged,
round-bodied, opulent
as vowels & perfectly
wingéd—each strikes
the pose *passé juvenile
delinquent* on driftwood
in the gallery's open aviary.
Dear Catastrophe Waitress
pipes in as the artist
with chevrons buzzed
into his scalp is treed
by art hounds, chatty as
sportscasters, erudite as
olives with their one red
point. The artist, it seems,
has mismanaged
imperfection, each of his
flighty objects accumulating
zeros. But what of these
thrushes? So hollow...
as if each were a vessel
for this character
I now inhabit
briefly, discretely, as I
peruse & genuflect, each
red second sabotaging
the previous, scavenging
& salvaging, trained
socially to chirp no
grievances aloud against art

nor artist, goodly as any
obeisant deacon. It seems
the birds are teaching me
how to watch them...
or watch myself from within.
Here a critic's ear
bends sail toward another
conversation, hooks
a theory from an adjacent
squabble, & adopts it as his
own, & I cannot help
but be humbled
by these slippages, by
centuries of contradiction
in service of the new,
& I slip into some smaller
voice, performing other,
as the garden thrushes,
almost human now,
collect the dust
of our captivity.

TATTOOS

This garden thrush
ginning bees
from the hibiscus
articulates a relationship
between memory & desire.
Or doesn't. Best to watch.
Bird returns
from the bush
unrepentant, un-alone,
wings fraught
with a terrible music—
& a few new alarming,
living tattoos—
& proceeds
to seed from itself
the stinging subjects
of its desire
in a violent,
quotidian dance.
What memory of its
hunger, I wonder,
remains?
Are the stings
it endured
linked in its mind
inextricably
to satiation?
Would the accidental
prick of a stem or thorn
leave it ravenous?
Not a penance,
but a purchase.
Does it regard

its instinct thoughtfully,
as a kind of necessary
madness, perhaps,
like the woodpecker
who one day wakes
to slip its tongue
around its brain
(this is true)
& drive its virgin beak
into a sabal palm tree?
Desire lives
in dissatisfaction,
unable to ever taste
its unsuspecting hunger-
to-action casualty.
(Once desire claims,
it vanishes.)
Opportunity,
however illusory,
drives us wild
& flitting
about the fetish
symbols
of the enticement.
It reinvigorates one's
faith in the pure instant,
free of before & after-
math. Like memory
it usurps one's willingness
to participate, arriving
unannounced
with swift
appetite to explode
the immediacy of a moment.
We cherish this
lack of agency,
rejecting self-authorship,
& are emptied

of time's form—
an ache
blossoming
into the shape
of our want.
Desire (umbilicus)
unites us to thrush,
thrush to bee,
bee to flower,
whose own petal
dismisses its bond
with the calyx
for the intractable
quick love
of
gravity.

EVERY TIME YOU SMILE, I SMILE

*Aorat*OS*

This garden thrush
(née song thrush) is a lark,
      an experiment
in materialism, an attempt
to determine how-when-
why the mind bends
      to the ephemeral.
Imagine this bird exploded
        so far & so fast
the migration of its atoms
     become both
an anachronistic wave
& quanta of pointillism—
  light from a dying star.

      (Finely layered
in space-time, existing
somewhere between
the fleeting neutrinos
         of Seurat—
ascertainable only
when striking
      at something larger—
& the polarizing Ben Day
      dots of Lichtenstein,
haunting some immense vacuity
& charging the in-between.)

Where then lies its song?

     Some other poet
has been here.
I have the records—song,

84

poem, memory:
['Split the Lark & you'll
find the Music / Bulb
after Bulb in Silver rolled.']
Dissected for its expression,
the bird, with study,
disappears,   & with sifting
its particles expand
to be viewed no longer
irrelative
of everything else,
reconstituted as collective
probability   or the self-
fulfilling replications
of a viewer-cum-creator.
Matter as energy
as meaning, both testament
& dream, the *either-or*
of immemorial, & we—
irreverent, unshakable—
operating
as but the slightest exaggeration
in tone.

HICCUPS

Hyps*OS

This garden thrush, grub
fat, notices me watching,
notices me not

Wine cork popping—some
breeze lilts a dandelion—
garden thrush at noon

Brooklyn lamp—garden thrush
caught beneath the cyclist's tire
still twitters, still sings

Drunk off its own heartbeat,
stroking clavicle of moon—
garden thrush bewitched

COSMICOMIC QUESTOR

Ich*OS

This garden thrush
is the infinite syllable
held   [...]
possibly some
bequeathed sentiment
or an essential call
a prolonged naming
Dear Unified & Infinite
Interim you are a god's
stalled instruction
finger at the lip
first thought or final wish
Dear Saint Vacuum
of Interminable Silence
& Forgetting you are
Reason's longest winter
false prophet of hope
that words can outlive
us listeners
with Time peering back
unblinking as a tanked tiger
shark I feel moved to repeat
your frozen vocalization
a music of energy creator &
destroyer it moves me
to examine my own singsong
& surreptitious love
for the failure that precedes
those sounds sexing themselves
into poetry the syllable as
shadow effigy
              it takes a pairing
to rush in & revive it

another word/sound
thrush
thrush
thrush *plush*   [...
this garden thrush
plush as a rush of barbiturates
crux of the coroner's kingdom
unhinged as religion's engine
itinerant as wind twitch
of the slinky dominatrix
unleashing forgiving permission

plush
this second utterance
an act of will
to become beyond
the first's cry of being
this a gift a giving way to
a season a song for one's
pleasurable aperture
of private performance
sans raison d'être

o wrong wrong-headed
long-winded whisperers
music can be meaning
enough
o long song-laden words
you are reason enough
for reason's artful
obliteration

PLACEBOS

This garden thrush
is garnering burrs
as it escalates
through the brush,
is garnering bits
as it unfurls
across my computer
screen, digitized &
greedy in its becoming,
claiming, pixel by pixel,
its birthright
in code & magnetic fields.
The old world snaps.
The new physical
arrives in diminished
consciousness,
built to please
& with a bionic taste
for the graphic
element it will next
inherit, hungry.
Narcissus at the water's
edge sees his truer,
eternal self—pliable,
reducible,
downloadable,
& made new.
The movie star
is made of extras.
The morning star
implies no North.
What zodiac
could possibly contain

what it is itself
contained within?
What inner life
will we admire
once we decode
ourselves
and replace I
with arch-I
in archive?

THE WESTERN DISTRICT

*Ka*OS*

This garden thrush
walks into a bar
with a cat on a leash
& a flamingo in drag.
The bartender asks him
what's the deal with
the entourage.
The garden thrush says,
"My grandmother died
& willed me this old lamp,
& when I go to clean it,
out pops this genie,
who says he'll grant me
three wishes.
So I asked for a bird
with long legs
& a subservient pussy."
The garden thrush
loses it, squawking
at his own joke.
The bartender goes back
to wiping mugs
with a rag. The garden
thrush asks the bartender
what the problem is
& the bartender says,
"Jesus, T. This shit,
day in day out? Where'd
you get these two?"
T looks over his shoulder.
"Met 'em at a party. What's
your fucking problem?"
"Go home to your kids, T,"
says the bartender.
"Not before I get a drink,"
T replies.

"We really gonna do this?"
asks the bartender.
The garden thrush stares
at the bartender a moment
before putting on his hat.
"Some kind of brother,"
he says.
"It aint no pleasure in life,"
says the bartender.
"Fuck you," says the garden
thrush. "It aint nothin'
but pleasure."

"Is that guy really your
brother?" asks the flamingo
once they're outside.
"We served together," says
the garden thrush.
The cat is already down the block.
"Served? Served like how?"
asks the flamingo. "Like at
a Burger King? Like in a war?
You aint been to no war."
The garden thrush leans
against the wall, points.
"When you tuck that
between your legs,
you reckon that makes you
more of a woman
or less a man?"
The flamingo has heard enough,
takes flight, an asterisk tagged
to the moon. The garden
thrush opens his flask,
wishes he had back all that
money spent on shrimp
cocktails. Imagines
the flamingo's ruffled
chest, the questioning neck
& articulate pink thighs.

This pleasure...it could be
mine, he thinks, but I've got
no right to pleasure. I've got
no right to a fucking thing.
What good am I? What's the point?
I just help other people feel better
about not being me. A good time
for a short time, & hell after.
Misery, delayed by laughter.
A sacrifice here & there
& you're left with nothing
to sacrifice. & anyone with nothing
to sacrifice is no one at all.
No one at all, aint that
right, brotherman?

He contemplates a final wish
& wanders back toward
the eastern district,
his voice haunting
the ridiculous streets:
　"Hi diddly dee, on-board
　I met the Reaper!
　Hi diddly doe, he asked me
　Who should go!
　Hi diddly do, I told him
　about you!
　Hi diddly dang, you told him
　the same thing!
　As for my love of Reapers,
　son, he is my brother's keeper.
　As for my love of brothers, boy,
　we'll meet up in the ether."

V.

Ode to the MQ-9 Reaper

ODE TO THE MQ-9 REAPER

*Log*OS (circa 2010-2012)*

I.

(I dreamt you up in third grade.) Ultra-cool & promo slick, a predatory dart
zip-lining threads of nimbi, unmanned, over darkling continents, your bot-brain
a paragon of focus & yet mechanizedly desireless, as self-aware as silverware,
& thus incapable of cruelty when delivering laser-guided missiles calibrated
to fountain a small bus full of explosives into a contained puff above a crowded
marketplace, or slip eel-like through a cave's oculate within the Hindu Kush.
Your blurry, thermal aerial view beset with squared crosshairs a rookie war
director's owlet dream: oblivious vermin swept up with gestural efficiency from
heights that confer the necessary filmic distance of omniscience, as if each strike
were a warrant fulfilled by reason abiding divine instruction: Michelangelo's
God fist-bumping Adam. Edited & packaged, a select few videoed assaults ship
to media outlets as evidence, an impressive staging intent to show a public what
humdrum work war's become—locate, track, eviscerate. Replicate. From these
spare scenes of bombed & reconfigured wreckages of cars & buildings ghosting
though a dusty plume arrives a satisfying vengeance for the loss of Sgt. Elias
from *Platoon*, those spry young Wolverines in *Red Dawn*, & my uncle's waking
battle dreams (of the Vietnam variety) that go unmentioned in advertisements
peddling the mastery of thumb-numbing single-shooter POV games for Xbox
& PlayStation as a skill set, with once implausible credits transferable to active
military duty. O to be gamers & destroyers, with each ethereal tick a countdown
aria to roadside decimation, or the anticipated signal of microwavable pizza—

I'm on YouTube again watching a task force seize a desert outpost, the offal
opulence of awful ordinance as witnessed by a documentarian's hand-held,
an eye unsteady in its capturing, but never insecure. By firefight an anecdotal
oral history begins developing its authors, these servicemen & -women who
user-posted comments identify as members of *Generation Kill*. Soldiers passing
soccer balls to poor kids an errant attempt to dupe a viewer into moral alliance
& engage the heart's surrender, but as the camera goes downrange, the images
shiver with heat & a sudden dubstep beat drops its discharge of epinephrine,
pumps us for the possibility of a shootout & invasive human plumage: gut-shots,

headshots, *Hajji* hematomas (& never a dead American), the BBC-style coverage devolving into Bang-Bang Club badassery, moments spliced for detachment via destabilizing rapidity. The first tank shot a Globe theatric to begin the operatic picaresque: *Pafghaniraq: the Musical.* Ubi sunt & heretofore? *Let the bodies hit the floor.* Dulce et decorum est? *You wanted in and now you're here. / Driven by hate, consumed by fear.* The tanks roll in, the tanks roll out. But Reaper, where they cannot go, you can—& suddenly we're Superman! Eye in the sky, womb with a view. You whizz to the rescue, my childhood A.I. dream's apotheosis as *M.Q. Joe*, as a voice narrating the hunt regurgitates post-Towers ideologies— the kind of stuff we get from news sources instead of news—& a superstructure emerges, with themes equating book learnedness with subversive otherness, & might with right, which Heaven atones, advocating our patriotic, righteous will-to-power.

& I get why we heart the hype. Your sleek iBomb design is *haute Apple* adorable: the extended wingspan, the ball turret cam. Viewed full-frontal, Hellfire missiles hang loosely clamped to the horizon of your asterisk body, itself a fusion of X-Wing Fighter & a *Lambda*-class Imperial Shuttle from *Star Wars*, a sexy sort of curvilinear Geek Goddess whose forehead slope recalls the stately dolphin fish, rear propeller the whirr of a rubber-banded planophore. Behold our Indian Springs Sphinx, riddled with weapons. But your work is deadly serious: to split atmospheres & genealogies alike, & do to human beings what bunker busters do to basements. In my child's mind you were precise, able to de-install a dictator as effortlessly as any computer virus, a typed command & *poof,* *democracy*. But the reality is always trickier: while 'bugsplatting' the enemy you also kill civilians, & often, a fact that crass reporters reduce to food metaphor (*in order to make an omelet*) & zealots to allegory (*God makes his omelets with American cheese*), but a truth remains: when targeting al-Qaeda, jihadists, Taliban, ISIS, you snatch the heads off schoolchildren. Actual little kids, with families smothered in radii of blast circles & a bloody sampling of bystanders. The Brookings Institution puts your civilian-to-militant kill ratio in Pakistan at 10:1. Possibly. New America Foundation says 1:6. Maybe. Actual numbers unavailable. I click from collateral damage to Google Maps, satellite zoom to downtown, & comb rooftops for the faintest fraction of your form hovering Ground Zero because I've read you minnow those twin blue columns of memorial light as New York's newest National Guard. I can't help but imagine what future recon missions Cuomo might commission. Will you one day sweep & clear meth labs? Will you whistle just above our neighborhoods, a goodly beat cop who when alerted turns bag snatchers into smatterings of gore a blogged cartoon Giuliani might welcome as graffiti? Or would you just zap terrorists?

& could we as Americans stomach accidents? A collapsed school gym, a Park Slope bar, the IFC, NYU, or BAM? In my dream you spiral slowly overhead in a droning corona of mechanized security, attentive as any parent. Are you the border patrol or the border? In your harmonious hum I hear George Carlin proselytizing on flamethrowers, a confluence of human ingenuity (*How do I throw fire from here—*) & what our culture embraces as a necessary wickedness (*—on people over there?*), as if the bargain struck with sentience was having to fulfill its graver innovations. Will the ramifications of your exploits serve as a parable, or dictate foreign policy? Do robot assassins outstrip the honor of our enemy, or us? This is not, I think, an academic question, unless we really wish to own the role of a global hobgoblin, dining expansively at the expense of others, crematoriums stirring in our cocktails.

II.

As a boy sweating it out in the swampy Florida ruins of the Space Coast, I conceived also the Extreme Frisbee, which when tossed onto a lawn levels a concentric blast horizontally, mowing the yard & thus finishing my chore, an easy circumvention of a nagging task I found torturous in humidity. Would the Air Force be interested in my toy version of the "daisy cutter"? It's unnerving, three decades in the rearview, my easy fascination with destruction. I can't say if it was fed by video games, toons, the assumptive natural tendencies of boys, or incidental fallout from grandparents who worked for NASA at the Cape, where I once met Ronald Reagan during an era of Cold War initiatives—rockets, satellites, weaponry, plutonium payloads; beach protesters' signs reading: *We Want to Grow Not Glow!* At ten I watched the shuttle Challenger craze a curious Y overhead as we paused in playing duck-duck-goose on the school's soccer field, our harmless game made instantly ridiculous, sickening perhaps, to our teachers, though I'd rather imagine our sport as analgesic to the abrupt cracks forming in their logic, a hopeful premonition (even as they instantly foresaw a future of layoffs & foreclosures, ransacked tourism & a raised crime rate, an anti-Oz ushered in by faulty O-rings) of enduring life—which touches me now, resting on this bench in McCarren Park & watching a group of latino kids batting around a diamond, a few of whom might one day serve overseas. In this Spring of uprisings & genocide & war—baseball. A juxtaposition one may enjoy like an itch on the back of the throat. But a better part of living is loving what we have worked & fought for when we can afford the having of it. Some say we fight for this opportunity alone. Others say to fight at all perverts the having. I see the boy pitcher catching the HEAT end of an RPG-7 in a few years, & think, *Play ball. Enjoy this having.* I worry, Reaper, you're nothing but the latest incarnation of defensive bulwark designed to keep our

leaders from having any skin in the game, a flying watchtower for One-Percenters.
But that's my irreverence speaking, as it's obvious you were designed primarily
as punctuation, a stop-gap for sentences like, "I'm going to plant an atomic bomb
(Reaper) in (Reaper) your (Reaper) city." & to keep young adults from shipping out
& having to bear the brutal brunt of difficult decisions. But I find the remoteness
of your remote control indicative of certain opaque policy makers, a reticence toward
disclosure adopted by governments & gatekeepers (fretful as any circus flea-handler)
who decide some truths are just too harsh/heady/hairy for a public. Your lofty hands-
off approach feeds into that, & I imagine a subsequent generation envisioning war
as raining droplets onto water beetles—bloodless because we do not see the blood,
effortless because we do not see the effort—& so a simpler thing than the arduous
recurring task of engaging in diplomacy. A not-so-futuristic, non-irregular Tuesday:
coffee, WiFi iTunes, Netflix *South Park* reruns in an open tab, your successor drone
narrowing on its target, requests a confirmation, & is approved by the same sugared
finger that seconds ago tested the relative squishiness of two types of jelly donut.

III.

Here's a line announcing a strong desire to reference Blue Oyster Cult in this poem,
or pepper in a bit more humor for digestion, but the shitstorm in my head's pushing
my levity button sublingual as my mammalian cortex indexes lines for a Codex
(disseminating tips on how to better agitate an ulcer) entitled *Driving a Blunt Point
Down a Dark Road, With a Wandering Eye for Wildlife & a Certain Recurring Fear.*
Dear Reaper, I interrogate to better know aspects of myself, it seems. My inquiry
into the meaning of your presence has made for incessant consternation, ineffective
sleep, a line by Karl Krauss my rare dreaming's epigraph, "In case of doubt, choose
in favor of what is correct." & around me the world becoming a sudden dustbin for
metaphors, e.g., these El Beit coffee cups stacked into one another lip-to-lip like
largemouth bass of similar size attempting to swallow whole their counterparts,
perhaps the symbolic error of my arrogance, choking on a subject more immense
than my wheedling could wend; a caricature, an enigmatic reach beyond my grasping.
Outside June ferments its special brand of Brooklyn light, summoning dog-walkers
& buskers & strollers to the park overlooking the motley chopper barges of the East
River & Manhattan's bric-a-brac skyline, & all the stylized lines I've erased in pursuit
of you are monumental failings I can't shake, & share with friends over café beers
& small plates of chorizo & applesauce, speaking of guilt for having not reached an
ethical conclusion of you, as my internal editor broods & kicks, distrustful of poems
that approach polemic, & rightly so. I could bend like the palm tree, ruffled

by opposing winds, yet breaking neither way; or play the twin-faced Janus who, given variations on a score, sings a garbled contrapuntal tune. But still each night I return to you, clouded with resentment, the questions I pose echoing as personal indictments: If I accept you as a net positive, must I then accept the death penalty, for which the cohesive moral arguments by either side I find by turns compelling & absurd? When if anytime is absolutism, in law or life, viable? & what of fallibility, stamped on every birth certificate? Is human error error's most humane defense? If war (as the poor) will always be with us (or us), should preemptive forgiveness accompany any loyalty we bestow upon our government, however begrudgingly? Is skepticism our better patriotism? *Resuming, marching, ever in darkness marching.*

IV.

The case made for your creation was utilitarian, with a catch. As an instrument sacrificing nothing of itself, you are a tool, Reaper—a dumb bucket of brimstone & nothing more. But in your work there's sacrifice, to be sure. Not the mundane daily forfeits made by people carving out their own identities with virtues like humility & patience—a guile amounting to a certain manufacturing of spirit— but with swift certitude in servitude, sacrificing the lives of others in our name. To deprive war of warfare's casualties (on our side, of course)—its main malignant property (to paraphrase Žižek)—is reiterated as your goal, & yet civilian casualties excluded from military updates discount the lives of victims whose freedom we're told is in part the reason why we fight, no? Surely *liberation* doesn't mean from life. Or are we expected to believe their desire for democracy (if indeed this is desired) denotes a predilection, an implicit willingness, for self-sacrifice in service of a greater good, this devotion somehow empirically antithetical to that of suicide bombers? ಠ_ಠ. #OverheardInDC. To usurp a suffering voice with ventriloquism or shush it with cover-up is the handiwork of dictators, dickheads, & directors of propaganda. A modicum of respect is paid by invoking a revoked life when reporting a victory, losses both targeted & untargeted. Shame is America's great barometer: it lets us know when we've crossed a line. Recall LBJ's reaction to Cronkite's condemnation of troops in Vietnam. We know sacrifice well enough: we've seen our citizens endure batons & hoses, suffer the lunacy of cops & crowds, or the indignity of being unjustly jailed & even murdered in the fierce nonviolent battles of giving of oneself. But what do you relinquish, Reaper? What do we lose by using you? Your advocates serve up spin like hors d'oeuvres—buttery, but with a bitter aftertaste—as detractors clamor eagerly for central space on aggregate news sites, Op-Ed columns marginalized & funneled through the foreign press. Each time you slip across an international border illegally to snuff a serial killer, the debates erupt, each side tending garden with the unimpeachable words of our forefathers, proven pesticides for fighting any weed or rhizome of rebuke. On the airwaves Senators, Representatives, & talking heads unite to enact a dance of prefabricated sound bites & slogans a Fifties adman might concoct to ameliorate "the befuddled masses," teaching us where to focus our newly engaged feelings: on the nationalistic *Pride* for our military's *Ingenuity*; the *Bravery* in making these difficult *Choices*; the *Talent* & *Teamwork*; the restored *Honor* in having doled out *Justice*. Phrases that imbued with righteous overtones subdue & collapse their subject, trivialize with jargon the power of authentic expression, & with the pompous authority of the politico, attribute a successful campaign to our fighting spirit, heaven-forged & exclusively American. Well firstly, Senator, nice tie. Lieberman called & wants his smirk back. & so we're clear, I find it slightly fucking irksome to be addressed as a collaborator in some monumental decision in which I had no direct say, & livid because I have a stake. In your speech against the enemy, are we the jurors, or the injured seeking justice? Looking out into the cameras, do you imagine the solemn, braided faces of a million confessors staring back, each troubled by a grief only your full pardon could relieve, being as we share in this responsibility? Do you stick to boilerplate clichés because language is a terminal for vagary & connotation, & our polling preferences remain a known unknown? Even if I shared your plan of action, the rhetoric smacks of self-glorifying punditry, as if you'd commandeered the bomb yourself & rode the goddamn thing to earth like Major Kong. This aint you vs the hippie-dippies, so stop trying to out-man-handle gravitas. One dead Head doesn't curtail much less abolish a terrorist movement, so let's talk turkey: the drone tactic of picking off bad guys one by one is feasible but expensive ($3k/hr); they're prone to crashes, slip-ups, have a flight hang-time of *Space Jam* Jordan on two days' rest & methamphetamine, & are practical merely as an application for hunting higher-ups who've had their covers blown by errant errand boys—a strategy that relies on runs-walked-in-on-balks to win. If it boils down to body count, Senator, let's discuss the flimsy bags of foulness: the body, as person, conflux of ideas, protein chains in congregation, a thin material: not the kind we halyard up a pole or drape over a coffin, but a living instance we either value or devalue with our actions. To keep the number of combatants-to-civilians killed out of your podium romp & rhapsody amounts to whitewashing in the name of foreign relations, does it not? (No need to wake the Far Right Czar-side of Karzai.) If ever our leaders & .gov devalue bodies, undermining each our own mind's dominion, we'll lend our heart's ears & eyes elsewhere, to be clued in by what vanguard follows the tag-team comic smackdown of Stewart & Colbert, the nebulous panopticon of WikiLeaks, or the ambitious wave of Anonymous grey-

hat hackers who post their findings online mere ticks after your talk. Transparency
is a form of objectivity, & truth a noumenon: by this I mean, we know bias exists,
so share your bias, & allow us to judge its worth. We need to know those running
our machines are functioning well, as well, & in good service. We need to know
that even if wars find us unavoidably involved, as with an attack on our harbors,
or a match scratched across Europe, though there may never be consensus, clarity
at least will guide our certainty in how we will advance & why & at what cost.
Make no mistake, your exploits (grave music) attract songbirds & whistle-blowers:
smartphone photojournalists, bloggers on crusade, a child's text arriving on devices
instantaneously. To stubbornly refuse to share with your constituents the hard facts
& steer clear from implementing policies marshaling forthrightness, you lose a not-
negligible portion of public trust; & find it worthwhile: as popular feedback during
election cycles could consign a $10 million Unmanned Aerial Vehicle (UAV) deemed
ineffective to the scrap heap. Phrases meant to assuage us, detailing the perils of
compromised National Security, would be fair *if* we'd requested preliminary attack
coordinates, communication logs, data that endangers operatives, etc., but what
most are after is POTUS' justifications (heavily footnoted), a casualty count, &
an honest conversation. Bear in mind what roosts in darkness awakens in darkness.
Some folks, unable to parse fact from fiction, feeling resentful, duped, & mishandled,
will invest attention, energy, & money in commiserating charlatans who entertain
conspiracy & preach a radical, bigoted, insular fascism that fetishizes your failures,
Senator. It's sad to watch such distrust flourish. It frustrates me, upends my mental
furniture. When folks demand what lecherous voices demand they demand of you,
it will be in equal measure to what they feel you've withheld. On all sides, animosity
for government grows, the perception being it conceals only to illustrate its power.
Evidence itself must be evidenced. Clamoring for graphic images of our own war
dead are the people who sought out pics of bin Laden's corpse (& Saddam's gallows
plunge, captured by a grainy camera phone; & Qaddafi beaten & sodomized
& hood-strapped like a deer & driven through the angry streets), if not to placate
their own disbelief, momentarily, then to finalize another draft of current history.
Perhaps it's fair to push past tastefulness & ask for images of our fighting dead;
those who suggest it could prompt fewer military actions are probably correct,
but then expect a surge in websites devoted primarily to gruesome battle porn,
with faces recognizable—an unfiltered horror show no PBS documentary by Burns
could fully mitigate for mass consumption, nor a le Carré novel stew in its juices,
feeding out the pearls. Some things can be engaged but not encapsulated; slip our
definitions; shift their natural structures when being observed, making it difficult
to weigh the potential outcomes of any approach. Shock weds us to understanding,

& sometimes mothers empathy (or trauma), & empathy activism, or a paralyzing awe, aware how little we can help. Shock enjoys the lifespan of a fruit fly, empathy the fig wasp, yet pitted in each, abuzz, a plot for ultimate change. If nourished too frequently by either, however, we numb to them. But if left unfed in intervals, we risk fostering conditions for bleak distortions of the soul, the rank solipsism of corruption, fear-mongering, isolationism, genocide. Best I think to arm ourselves with compassion, a word for love's morality, & an activity to be pursued to the point of effortlessness. To share in the suffering of another (our enemy (our idea of our enemy)) gives us a stake in their welfare & survival, our shared breaths & burials. This isn't breaking news. *History is a coroner's cold slab / the rise & fall of nations on display / & though the body is a bloody mess / its examination brings clarity.* So what does it matter what wrapping we box our rationalizations in, or the fingered reason we ribbon our bows about, if peace is the desired end result? & we cannot have peace without understanding. If the other suffers, we must suffer knowing. If it's wrong, we stop.

V.

The soldier relinquishes his body for the greater body. The conscientious objector relinquishes her body for the greater body. The terrorist relinquishes his body for the greater body. The martyr relinquishes her body for the greater body. Reaper, you relinquish nothing but another's body & our name. You respect not & want for nothing, & if by terrible error you misfire, you have no hands for blood to be on.

VI.

When Abraham took his only son Isaac to carry wood up Mount Moriah, which Samaritans (of the good ilk) believe was Mount Gerizim, in the West Bank, to do what his god had commanded, which was to bind his son & slit his throat, for proof of loyalty, it was always easy to imagine the scene as developed for Hollywood, a Warner Brothers production, where the complexities of devotion, split between familial love & a higher purpose, could be played out by actors we admired, whom we knew the studio would never allow to die onscreen, under a purpling sky & thunder & broad orchestral strokes that signaled a grave decision & torment of the spirit. What's more difficult to imagine is how a country father could make that climb up a path of white rock, fig & olive trees arriving in clumps, air smelling of the herbs of his own childhood, perhaps—oregano, thyme—these brambles at his feet, as his son asks, repeatedly, what it is they are planning to sacrifice using all this wood, & having to hold that secret in for the whole duration, which would feel like an infestation of the brain, knowing the hot knife at his thigh will soon be under his son's chin, the smooth skin found there, & that he will have to puncture or slit or in some way force this tool into this boy in a manner that would bleed him out like a goat, not yet knowing some force will stop him, knowing only that to do this he must prepare himself, empty himself of feeling & so become that tool of his lord, given to the invisible hand, & sacrifice himself in order to sacrifice his son. & what child, tucked under the covers, listening as their own father reads this bedtime story to them from a book opened many times before, doesn't imagine themself Isaac?

VII.

Recently, among the industrial vestiges of Bushwick, I found myself in a white box some entrepreneurial do-it-yourselfers had carved into an art gallery, & found mixed in with the post-grad work informed by the subtle forms of Lin & Beuys, the hard-wrought whimsicalness of Anderson & Baldessari, two flat screen TVs hanging side by side on the wall, where I watched a fluttering arthropod buzz onlookers in McCarren Park as the other screen detailed its aerial imaging as layered onto a satellite view of Google Maps. As chance would have it, the artist was there & gave me a rundown of his work. *I saw this in a dream*, I said, feeling slightly ridiculous. *Me too*, he said. *I'm intrigued by drones*, I said. *It's all that I can think of*, he said. The drone was strung above us, its articulated exoskeleton & elbow cameras not quite so menacing in repose. Onscreen we watched it wobble along a swarming path remotely set by iPhone. *It won't need you soon*, I said. *That's the point*, he replied. *How long did it take to design?* I asked. *It's a kit*, he said. *You can buy your own online.* I told him of this poem, how in using a received form, an irregular ode (which I've wrecked) to receive your form, I'd moved beyond a place of comfort & the sonic permutations of lyric wanderlust I usually trust to gather what it grows, & into a mode of formal speculation. *These things will do that to you*, he said, as if I were hard-wired to follow tension to intention. *Why just last week a company approached me asking if I could outfit this thing with a thermal cam.*

VIII.

The Terra Wasp. The Aqua Wasp. The Gnat. The Raven. The Fire Scout. The Dragon Eye. The DarkStar. The Desert Hawks. The Gray Eagle. The Global Hawk. The Hunter. The Sentinel. The Prowler. The Shadow. The Predator. The Reaper. The Avengers.

T e Terra Wa p. T e Aqua Wasp. T e Gnat. T e Raven. T e Fire Scout. T e Dragon Eye. T e DarkStar. The Desert Hawks. The Gray Eagle. The Global Hawk. The Hunter. The Sentinel. The Prowler. The Shadow. The Predator. The Reaper. The Avengers.

qua patet orbis—
dehydrated wreaths on rose-
water–colored sand.

The Terra Wasp. The Aqua Wasp. The G p The G t. The R av . The F e ut. T e   ag n E e. T e   a k tar. T e   e ert awks. The Gray Eag e. The Gl al Hawk. The Hunter. The Sentinel. The Pr wler. The Sha   w. The Pre ator. The Reaper. The Avengers.

The avatar will enter the theater	(The geek test egg)
a theater: trawler of heaven,	(The punk egret)
Shakespearean thug.	(Ghastly went the twerp)

The Terra Wasp. The Aqua Wasp. The Gnat. The Raven. The Fire Scout. The Dragon Eye. The DarkStar. The Desert Hawks. The Gray Eagle. The Global Hawk. The Hunter. The Sentinel. The Prowler. The Shadow. The Predator. **The Reaper.** The Avengers.

IX.

The line "(Ghastly went the twerp)" was first conceived as "(Petty wrath, this length of West)," among other improbable incarnations, plus or minus a few switched-out letters; ultimately I chose the former to fit an evolving characterization of you as unexpected bird of prey. Treating the historical list of drones as layered anagram was just another attempt to chip you from stone, a time-intensive experiment to hone (home) in on the idea of you using a formal device of creative constraint not unlike meter, or a Matthew Barney bungee chord. & if by certain measures it fails, I'll accept that. But let it be a failure with transparency: here are my word choices, here a soliloquy trope that allows for this presence of mind, the delights & false turns I've made, the frictions & fractious phrasing & varying musics. & this stanza of *Kora in Hell*-ish afterthoughts is part of that. Relationships need their breathers, their steps back, in order to assess what has been achieved, what is still at stake; it's exhausting, this swarm technique I've employed to both encapsulate & out you. I've heard *Moby-Dick* described as Melville's own attempt to capture in language the whale's essential 'thingness'—fleeting form, elusive essence—by framing events preceding & surrounding its hunt, its hunters' histories, & the industry relying upon its animal fats & oils. We get a minor telling of its impact, & sense the authorial hand creeping in at the sides. He divulges the secrets of its anatomy, charts its behavior in an attempt to elucidate a nature, collects salty anecdotes & myths to better keep it buoyed about a surface of referential symbolism. & still the whale evades totality; the trap is tripped but nothing caught. Where in a whale exists a whale? What core thingness among parts? If not a sum of facts & traits & qualia, if irreducible to cross-section, if un-pin-down-able by narrative, imagistic, or lexical triangulation, then how does one account for it? It is a phantom object: the closer you look, the less you see. Melville must have enjoyed the slip of it, lurching at so many angles. *Gospel of Ishmael, Book of Second Job*, a testament concerning a depleted man conspiring to kill what he cannot capture nor contain: not a physical Leviathan, but a bitter logic of injustice & vengeance trafficking within. Had Ahab early on harpooned his psyche's cachalot, wrenched the jaw from it, flensed & minced it & laid it bare before maritime birds who'd take it in their gullets & disperse, his crew & himself might have lived longer, but then we'd be left with no lesson by which to mark our moral lives, which shows the truer whale for which Melville used Ahab as the bait, & for which I use Melville, so that a discussion might invoke possession, & the impossibility of possessing you. & I say it aloud to myself, & say it another way, that language is mere iron fillings betraying a magnetic field, exposing one aspect of a thing (a force) by its properties. I desire but will never hold the atomic fact of you in my brain. You are too quick & I lack the stamina, the knowledge, the knowhow. I use imperfect tools. In the end I have just myself alone in a room with words & images, & hope of their effectiveness.

***

To begin with this:

Writ into its programming a complex theory of the heavens & the earth, & a mystical treatise on the art of attaining truth; so that the Reaper in its own self was a riddle to unfold; a wondrous work in one volume; whose mysteries not even itself could read.

mindful of my own biases & beliefs:

This is what you've been shaped for, Reaper! to chase these white whales, for both sides of man, & under all sides of earth, until they spout black blood for Rolls, Infiniti, Audi.

while altogether trying to avoid this:

All that most maddens & torments; all that stirs up the lees of things; all truth with malice in it; all that cracks the sinews & cakes the brain; all the subtle demonisms of life & thought; all evil, to crazy Me [Your Humble Investigator] were visibly personified, & made practically assailable in the Reaper. He piled upon the Reaper's white hump the sum of all general rage & hate felt by his whole race from earliest ancestors down; & then, as if his chest had been a mortar, he burst his fucking hot heart's shell upon it.

X. General Characteristics of the MQ-9 Reaper Drone

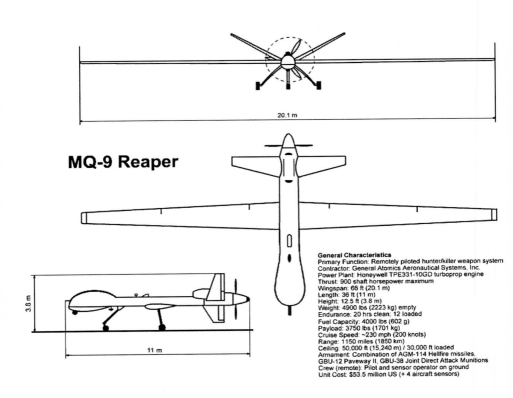

General Characteristics
Primary Function: Remotely piloted hunter/killer weapon system
Contractor: General Atomics Aeronautical Systems, Inc.
Power Plant: Honeywell TPE331-10GD turboprop engine
Thrust: 900 shaft horsepower maximum
Wingspan: 66 ft (20.1 m)
Length: 36 ft (11 m)
Height: 12.5 ft (3.8 m)
Weight: 4900 lbs (2223 kg) empty
Endurance: 20 hrs clean; 12 loaded
Fuel Capacity: 4000 lbs (602 g)
Payload: 3750 lbs (1701 kg)
Cruise Speed: ~230 mph (200 knots)
Range: 1150 miles (1850 km)
Ceiling: 50,000 ft (15,240 m) / 30,000 ft loaded
Armament: Combination of AGM-114 Hellfire missiles,
GBU-12 Paveway II, GBU-38 Joint Direct Attack Munitions
Crew (remote): Pilot and sensor operator on ground
Unit Cost: $53.5 million US (+ 4 aircraft sensors)

XI.

Personality strikes target specific high-level individuals. *Signature* strikes are strikes against suspicious confluences of people (suspected terrorists, sympathizers, training camps) based on vague factors like age & location. The bulk of strikes are Signatures. *Disruption* strikes are "crowd kill" Signature strikes operating with direct evidence of a threat to national security. For each type there is no opportunity for surrender. There is no due process. The dewdrop world is but a dewdrop world. & yet. & yet.

XII.

To realize the air purifier I've recently purchased to cleanse my house of dust particles comes from the same company (Honeywell) that designed your turboprop engine: Factory 1: Remotely piloted hunter/killer weapon. Factory 2: Relief for asthmatics.

XIII.

A poet-teacher of mine rolled in late for class once & sat, hands folded on the table we all shared, looking out upon us as if we were each Persephone in her garden, victims of a future kidnapping, & said, 'I've just read we're making nuclear weapons small enough to fit in suitcases. If there was ever a time to be arrested in protest, this is it.' & we each, separately & in unconscious unison, almost imperceptibly, did not move. Befuddled by the unreality of the news & our mentor's expectations, we weighed the pros & cons of sudden activism, anticipating an impulsive flash of filial courage even as we prayed for a collective cooling. Instead, dawdling & nodding agreeably, we opted out, dragging our naked helium heads from a smoggy cloud-cover of disgrace to embark upon the lessons of the day, of which there were many.

    This anecdote became the sort of chilly nugget I'd drop in a breakfast of bourbon after pulling an all-nighter trying to fashion from a complex idea ten pure syllables of poetry, & forego the snap of sleep for slow evaporation, having failed to seize the throated moment at its inspired impetus many hours earlier. Being a disciple of impulse & self-fulfilling prophecies—the sparks of revolution, I imagined—my failures left me feeling low, if not absolutely gutted. I'd chide myself for having resorted to bibliomancy of the classics (kernels of ideas I'd pot & shake over a blue flame) & crude word-pilfering from peers & websites (whose users coined ad hoc lexicons for instantaneous appropriation, riffed-off & punned-on by others, each an arbiter of a living language) instead of relying on my own internal devices: Mini-Hadron Connotation Collider, Hubble Logoscope. What gain was had trying to perfect a minor line? What readership lost or won? What impact? What decisive battle undercut in having not marched on the state capitol building that day to jerk a headline from some field reporter? Did I really lack initiative, or was it that I'm naturally skeptical of secondary sources? Had my crafting, the back & forth internal squabbling, sucked the marrow from a healthy, living organism? Did they ever make those goddamn suitcase bombs?

Atomic facts. How much of me, reduced, molecules rearranged, would constitute what percentage of you? If we are locked together in this natural world, of the same matter, am I responsible for your every aspect? I can't accept it. I couldn't sleep or eat an egg. I rely on borders, distinctions that separate. & yet I feel the friction of your movement. Any theory of surface contains an idea of edges, ends & beginnings, interference, commingling, restraint, subversion, how things touch & where. But here you are, albeit chemical, catapulting what amounts to lightning through my cell walls, & my imagination runs.

Any theory of surface depends upon which side of it you're on. I could sit here skipping stones all day. Or I could watch the flat side of some altogether alien subject collapse my sky in brilliant fashion, one realized blip at a time, until finally lowering to my closer investigation. Humans are surface in that we're both barrier & brane: a sovereign fortress of rectitude, when at defense; when carefree, about as permeable as rhubarb pie. When we are deep, we are as deep as what is there. *And nothing can exist except what's there.* But of course we're deeper than that, more than our reality, more than experiential filtration systems, materialism sifting through media. More than a sum of systems. My idea of you will always be more summary than sum, Reaper, even as I systematically uncoil the looping layers holding you intact, because you are the layers, & the intactness, & my desire to see you differently. I am conscious of this & yet persevere into possible idiocy. If you contain a spirit, it's our shared imagination. (Plump porcupine.) & you our Caliban: half demon heart, half twangling instrument of empire.

Consciousness exists, meaning the universe accounts for it, & so may use us, its fallible stumblebums, to better understand its own workings, in accumulative degrees; not some five-deck shoe of blackjack arranged to perplex the number counters, but a system unfinished, which a mode of sci-fi expressionism might one day examine & illustrate. To better understand itself, the mind revisits itself in memory. The college of correlatives, where we learn of interconnectivity. The mnemonic consulate, where we work each day at failing better. This is one understanding of progress—the arboreal dendrite in bloom, flowering receptors to receive at the synapse a radiant charge (which changes everything (shockwaves (of intelligence))). The desire for an apple, the apple in my hand. But before that, like a child's desire, the reach for what it cannot grasp. Then the grasping. To be or to be better at, & try not to be better at being worse. The memory of that learning. To better understand its own workings, the poem revisits itself through language. The impartial eye & itinerant image, how they syrup through each other's fingers, clinging each to each but never caught. How rhythm is both a wave & a trellis. How momentum expands a moment. How interruption & imperfections can tango & twist a critical mind from contempt to contemporary. How mutually exclusive ideas can intermingle in a single line without genuinely coalescing, & then in the memory genuinely coalesce. To better understand his own workings, the poet works. The blank page is a plank as thick as his world, a baseline of knowledge he'll challenge to undermine. He wets & warps it, testing for weakness. The final form is unforeseeable, a boat or a rod, or a powder keg; he's probably just ruining wood. But it's good work, & the more he works at it, the better the bender. His travels are varied—Tokyo; his tinker's heart; as far as the neighborhood bar. He studies the work of other woodwarpers, wonders over his own porous specimen. A pale sort of thing. Mostly space, at a molecular level. He never knew he knew so very little. With one plank bent he grabs another. As big as his world, but now a bit bigger. The worries of work are rejuvenating. They ready him...for more work.

What infestation is music in language? It says all the time what I don't mean to want, & better. & concentrating on you has me staring at blue until all I can see now is yellow. When the youngling woodpecker first hammers its head into a tree, does it fear it's lost its mind?

I was reading Auden when the second war with Iraq broke out. Come a year later, *September 1* was everywhere on August 29th. *Imperialism's face / And the international wrong.* My friend J—— came by & we walked with the protesters up Seventh Avenue, a thousand flag-draped coffins tracking hundreds of thousands of demonstrators toward Madison Square Garden, where the Republican National Convention had set up shop, & where on its steps well-suited clusters of our ideological opposites (our organizers assured us) watched in muted ceremony as the polychromatic orgy of hordes passed by, trumpeting their pains & grievances & tacking their secular Theses of Demands to every eardrum in earshot. But even in that wash of unity there was infighting, bickering, bad-mouthing, brutes. We were as wary of each other as we were of them, & they were of us; our joined voices a loose architecture, a toupee the wind kept disheveling. As the crowd dispersed with calls for a socialist

paradise or a centrist uprising, & the catcalls of bankers who'd ruin us later, J——
& I kept walking all the way up to Central Park, to sit on the gray slope of Umpire
Rock overlooking the baseball fields, & discuss it all. *Was this for anything?* was
the question, & I had within me Auden & the memory of that class some two years
earlier, & figured yes, it was necessary, even as gesture or performance, because it
was if nothing else good work. *All I have is a voice.* "But what purpose does it serve
if it's just a party?" asked J——. Reaffirmation. A reminder of the work that came
before us. Of our own work. *From the conservative dark / Into the ethical life.* Those
that came came together to oppose a stupid war & unethical governing, spies & liars,
& even if we didn't agree on everything, we agreed on that. *May I, composed like
them / Of Eros and of dust, / Beleaguered by the same / Negation and despair, /
Show an affirming flame.* Earlier that day we'd been asked to carry a casket &
declined. I wanted to be free to wander. My friend felt a deep distrust of forming
any particular alliances, saying we should own our own perspectives, informed by
separate experience, & gather with those differences in mind. We left the boulder
& headed for the West Village, hungry & silent as we traced the fleeting afternoon
to its darker avenues, alone & not alone, & passed by 52nd Street, where in 1939
a British expat sat down in a dive bar & scribbled out, not a call to action, but some
observations on the horrid state of things; stealing glances at the other patrons;
finding in the mirror behind green alcohol bottles the smooth, pensive face *Life*
captured before it broke into waterfall; self-exiled from fame & its devotees; a lover
gone to California; & trying to drink through an internal argument, he came up
with this: *We must love one another or die.* & there you have it: a 32-year-old's stab
at encroaching fascism, sounding more like a borrowed Beatles pick-up line, or a verse
a precocious schoolboy might have penned, frustrated when other notes he sent
his heart's desire met only with cheery ambivalence. *We must love one another or die.*
It rings simplistic—the antidote for a threatening infection being the hope it heals
itself under a bandage of utopic, willed camaraderie; as if Nazis slaughtered for lack
of this. But the urgency behind the message feels genuine, & the dread that powers
a powerless individual to shake low-hanging fruit from a wilting How-the-Fuck-Can-
I-Stop-This tree may revitalize a desperate congregation. It's the antithesis of trying
to unring the bell of war with a few diplomatic lines that act as apolitical earplugs.
But even so, this plea for harmony was weirdly tardy: the storm had already begun.
The question was, what to do next? Should America get involved? Form a coalition?
Arrange a summit with the Germans? In this the poem is modest, as poetry is an
inquisitive art, lest one forget, & to supply each question posed with an ultimate
answer doesn't mean the poem is finished, just that the poet is. Finished. So Auden,
though perhaps unnerved that his adopted American kin appeared content to

drink away their relatively small concerns the very day Germany invaded Poland, stopped short of saying they should rise to the political demands of the occasion, or grow a global superego. After scouting the bar's bleak-bank of depressives, whom he counted himself among, I'd bet, he found *Lost in a haunted wood / Children afraid of the night / Who have never been happy or good.* Some might argue he soured to our species, but in the poem's snowballing antipathy & verbal antagonisms tallying our faults lies the poet's true challenge—that of capturing competing ideas in cognitive dissonance, & to test & augment his findings, keeping what resonates. No Bible tract but a sparring interaction, the fevered theater of a mind unsure of its own footing. To make an open case for war might have proven unforgivable, if only to himself; but to disregard a land-grabbing psychopath would be viewed, at best, as a clarion call for his supporters & detractors alike to roll up their sleeves. Confronted with blind alleys, the poet drove the moment inward, afraid & resentful of the fear, so he might tease from his own uncertainty what troubled him of Power & the pain inflicted in its pursuit. This mapping of the atmosphere sent his brain pinballing into buttresses supporting the more incendiary claim that we were not all in it together. Together in our wickedness & decency. Together in our shared reliance on one another, which amounts to shared responsibility. & so he left the reader to the dictates of her own conscience when determining what battlefields materialized from the page, the only certainty being that in navigating this model of a model world, one is never alone. & though over the years Auden altered this poem, calling it his worst, banning it from collections & anthologies because it felt dishonest, unfinished, unclear, it mattered very much to me—munching a slice from Joe's Pizza on Carmine Street, the dream of Camus' solidarity also eking its way in there between the peppercorn & basil, the salts & oils, people-watching through the open window & wondering if struggle is our human glue, & if we build our culture largely the way be build ourselves, by wrestling with opposing views, even if some matches last a lifetime. The poem itself wasn't the protest. The walk down Seventh Avenue wasn't the protest. Our lives were the protest. Our galactic imperative of forward movement, our synapse songs & the good-work process of woodwarping. We will love without being told to. We will face our struggles & die.

XIV.

During the process of writing this last section, while my wife & I slept in the back room, someone crawled through the front window of our home (I can imagine him moving the garbage bins, smothering his smoke, slowly raising the window & in a sudden leap to his stomach, emptying himself into our lives) & stole among other things my computer. In my living room for maybe forty seconds, listening for my stirrings, & gone. & I know that if he (assuming it was a he) had made his way to my bedroom, with whatever intentions, & I had woken to find him there, I would have, I am sure of this, used the hunting knife I keep nearby to take from this stranger first what I would have been sure he was there to take from me.

(If by some means I'd been forewarned of his intent to break in &/or do me harm, would I have been justified in preemptively storming his house & murdering him? & what about his family, in order to eliminate all possibility of witness or retaliation, the Hatfield & McCoy strategy of mutual annihilation? Any offensive form of citizen self-defense (premeditated) is an indefensible offense, punishable by law—yet somehow acceptable if carried out by our military in a foreign land. & if it slips beyond the allotted time-frame, or leaks its secrets, we'll call it war. At my most cynical I'd say whoever attacks us gifts us a new opportunity to extend ourselves.)

But then, following the fracture: forgiveness. After weeks of piecing together what was lost, (what remains irretrievable: unsaved portions of this poem, partly memorized; the sense of our safety in this place) the fear & piss gave way, opening a space for reconstruction: parsing what was manageable & not, what could be mended or not, replenished or let go. Forgiveness is not forgetting, in my experience; it is an active occurrence of memory, to be reassessed in recollection. In this way, forgiveness is not a conclusion but an ongoing effort. & it is difficult, like any exercise, because it must again tear, like a muscle, what it aims to strengthen.

& here I forgive my intruder again. I'm no guard of moral decency, Reaper. In hounding you I've slobbered & frothed, chased my own tail, left a few nasty mistakes. & whenever the desire to excoriate & repudiate you finds another climax, I must reassess: today in Yemen, our "uneasy ally," 100 soldiers marching in a parade were undone by a single suicide. On YouTube a blue stampede of uniforms rushes from the bodies, & I think, if we are not the world police, we can at least be a global sibling. How do we fight this? Education, trade, lending, community building, construction, job training—it all takes time & costs run high in both money & blood. Without reform, the region faces dictatorial theocracy. But when their children grow, how will they remember this era, us, our actions? Our imprint should be small & productive. But for now, a Band-Aid: a quick track & flyby, & while you're out, snap us some close-ups of Socotra Island, that place looks crazy beautiful.

Reassess. I couldn't even keep the last sentence snark-free. Is the question, finally, what we choose to invest in, education or security? Reassess. An unrealistic goal should be our pursuit—a march toward imperfect instances. & when you fail, we must reassess your worth. They will not forget us; who knows what will be forgiven. Re-assess. Abdul-Rahman al-Awlaki for Anwar al-Awlaki. Reassess. Marine Staff Sergeant Jeremy Smith & Navy Hospitalman Ben Rast for Fahd al-Quso. Reassess. Warnings that children might be present, disregarded by our officers. Reassess. Little Fatima of Egypt, split by the Hellfire Romeo that killed Mustafa Abu al-Yazid. & here I forgive my intruder again. & flowering in me a stance tomorrow may crush.

But it's tomorrow, & it hasn't.

I speak from one side of a gulf, the side with power, the side kept safe. I believe you save lives, in that, for a time, you can hamper the options of our enemies. I believe you will be with us a long time to come. I believe you've made the future borderless. I believe those lacking power will gain power through you. I believe you will be used to terrorize us. I see no way around it.

"Right now, for about the cost of an iPad, a person could buy a used Parrot AR Drone, a radio-control 2.4GHz receiver, and a WiFi Yellowjacket, get a Ubiquiti PowerAP N router for the distance, a cloverleaf antennae, pack it with a small amount of explosives & hover it up to any floor of the UN you wanted. & you can do that from, hell, Roosevelt Island? Maybe even Gantry Park? You don't even have to be in Manhattan."

"But people have been flying toy helicopters for years & I've never heard of anything like that happening."

"We're in the infancy of this thing. Wait 'til these get faster & more stable. Wait until you've got a thrust-vectoring jet or quadrotor some 15-year-old maps out the specs for & posts online. You put a GPS onboard, set a timer, hide it on a rooftop, & drive to Maine for lobster & an alibi."

"& we'll retaliate. Go make a thing a nothing & call it peace."

"We don't even call it that anymore."

Thanks, online forum hobbyist. Let's go make coffee for the FBI.

XV.

& so, Reaper, after a year of watching you become our go-to weapon, our Big Gun, & as news of your travels travel & make news, on NPR, in the glossy covers of major magazines, after you were infected by your first virus, after Occupy Washington staged a rally outside General Atomics in DC, & as Iran decodes your captured sibling & scientists construct out of your ethos a robot hummingbird, I confess to finding in your present work no clear instance of what should be our greater plan— security in service of serenity. Not for dominance or disdain. Not for justice pursuing vengeance. Not for negotiating leverage. Not for show of power. Not for one & killing twenty. Not for not for. If poetry is news that stays news, I would rather this poem follow you headlong into obscurity, where you as the transfixed object & my words as what-will-suffice greet each other at a point of detonation above a thin, horizontal path to yield culturally & historically all the raw accumulative power of a hiccup.

If not, others will be along to bind you with law & word. Other watchers. Other woodwarpers. I see no real end to our progressive ropes.

It is raining on a Sunday. Children in flip-flops splash each other in puddles. My wife is playing the tongue drum I bought for her birthday. Outside my window, a lone gull of no consequence. Then gray, empty sky. No small luxury. We should get to the market before it closes.

NOTES

*OS=Operating system.

Odysseus Teaches One of His New Dogs to Say 'I Love You'
Upon returning home from war & adventure, Odysseus, up to that point feared dead, found his home full of greedy & lascivious suitors courting his wife. Dressed incognito as a beggar, Odysseus joined them even as he plotted their deaths, but was immediately recognized by one soul, his poor dog, Argos. Argos lay incapacitated in a pile of cow shit, too old even to stand, yet able to wag his tail a little. But Odysseus, fearful of being outed, strolled past his faithful companion without any overt acknowledgment, shedding instead a single tear, after which Argos promptly died.

Bedford Ave L
Dedicated to the memory of poet Joshua Basin.

Wall Street Confidential
A lot of this refers to the 2008 stock-market-slash-housing-market crash. Some acronyms: LEH—ticker for Lehman Brothers; EKG—Electrocardiogram; ARM—Adjustable-rate mortgage; RPG—Rocket-propelled grenade.

Tattoos
There's a part of me that enjoys letting poems find their way into un-truths, fantasy, false histories. Song thrushes eat snails, not bees, though mistle thrushes do, & that difference changed the poem. I loved how the original turned out, but even so, I wrote an alternative version:

This garden thrush
ginning snails
from the hibiscus
articulates a relationship
between memory & desire.
Or doesn't. Best to watch.
With an aerialist's
acrobatic unspooling, bird
returns from the bush un-

alone, unrepentant,
& proceeds to crack
on a stone's anvil
the protective shell
of its catch in a violent,
quotidian dance.
What does it remember,
having fed its hunger?
Does it regard instinct
as a necessary madness,
like the woodpecker
who one day wakes
to drive its perfect beak
into a palm tree?
Desire dies at the gates
of satisfaction, to be reborn
on the other side, as itself;
except in memory, where one
can want, have, have had,
the circuitous event absorbing
our re-absorption of it,
& we are fulfilled
by an essential emptiness.
Hunger: A Retrospective.
Recollection (our flight)
can reinvigorate one's faith
in the pure instant,
free of before- or after-
math, usurping even one's
willingness to participate,
arriving unannounced &
with swift appetite to explode
the immediacy of a moment.
To lose agency is to lose
a sense of self-authorship,
yet desire (umbilicus) unites:
us to thrush/ thrush to snail/
snail to flower, whose leaf

now dismisses its bond
with the calyx
for the intractable,
quick love
of gravity.

*

Also: "Split the Lark & you'll find the Music / Bulb after Bulb in Silver rolled" is a line
from Emily Dickinson. (One I can't seem to shake, as it appeared in another book of
mine, as well.)

THE FILM
All answers delivered by the crew in the interview section of The Film are derived from
letters taken from the original section in the order in which they first appeared, as
evidenced by the gray lettering. The director took as his stage name an anagram.

THE SCORE
Each successive section of this poem is comprised of deteriorating anagrams constructed
from the previous section, line-by-line, the third installment of which creates a passage
from *Alice's Adventures in Wonderland*. In further divergence, the final section utilizes
the lines from the first section run through at most 58 languages via a translation
engine (Google). The result was curated for content (halted at one translation, or
allowed to continue) but rarely edited, save for a few instances of articles transposed
for clarification. The generating languages were applied in the following order: English,
Afrikaans, Albanian, Arabic, Armenian, Azerbaijani, Basque, Belarusian, Bulgarian,
Catalan, Chinese, Croatian, Czech, Danish, Dutch, Estonian, Filipino, Finnish, French,
Galician, Georgian, German, Greek, Haitian Creole, Hebrew, Hindi, Hungarian,
Icelandic, Indonesian, Irish, Italian, Japanese, Korean, Latin, Latvian, Lithuanian,
Macedonian, Malay, Maltese, Norwegian, Persian, Polish, Portuguese, Romanian, Russian,
Serbian, Slovak, Slovenian, Spanish, Swahili, Swedish, Thai, Turkish, Ukrainian, Urdu,
Vietnamese, Welsh, Yiddish, & finally back to English.

THE PERFORMANCE
Inspired by a conversation with the performance artist, dancer, actor, & instructor
Karmenlara Ely.

QUASIMODOS
Dear Catastrophe Waitress is an album (& song) by Belle & Sebastian.

ODE TO THE MQ-9 REAPER

When I first began this piece, there was a major shortage of media reporting on drones. I relied upon a handful of journalists (a few of whom I reached out to) whose investigative work helped guide my thoughts regarding unmanned aerial vehicles, specifically: Scott Shane, Mark Mazzetti, Eric Schmitt, C. J. Chivers, Michael D Shear, James Risen, Christopher Drew, Jo Becker, Glen Greenwald, Jefferson Morley, Myra MacDonald, Michael Hastings, & photographer Noor Behram. A summary I wrote on the process of creating this poem, offering further explanation as to its origins, is available in *Epiphany Magazine*'s 2013 War Issue, in which this work first appeared.

"Ubi sunt" is short for "Ubi sunt qui ante nos fuerunt?" ("Where are those who were here before us?"). "Dulce et decorum est" is the title of an anti-war poem by Wilfred Owen, written in direct confrontation to Horace's "Dulce et decorum est pro patria mori" ("It is sweet & proper to die for one's country"). "Let the Bodies Hit the Floor" is a song by Drowning Pool, once used by American troops in Iraq & Afghanistan to psyche themselves up before heading out on their daily missions. The Slavoj Žižek paraphrase arrives from his essay "Passion: Regular or Decaf," & stands along with other comments made by him in various interviews. *Kora in Hell* is a hybrid work by William Carlos Williams. The three stanzas ending part IX are revamped paragraphs from *Moby-Dick*. The image used in part X owes its initial form to an anonymous poster on Reddit; I updated the info & altered the image for my needs. The poet-teacher in part XIII is the poet Robert Hass. This section also owes a good deal to poets Robert Browning, W.H. Auden, & Jorie Graham. Anwar al-Awlaki, Fahd al-Quso, & Mustafa Abu al-Yazid were each high-level al-Qaeda militants killed by UAVs; killed also by UAVs were Marine Staff Sergeant Jeremy Smith & Navy Hospitalman Ben Rast, as well as a young girl named Fatima along the Afghanistan-Pakistan border, as documented by photographer Noor Behram. The Parrot AR was the most popular quadcopter on the market at the time of this writing. The "thin, horizontal path" in the final section is a play off a John Ashbery line from his poem "What is Poetry?"

ACKNOWLEDGEMENTS

Thanks to my readers over the years: Wendy Millar, Joe Fletcher, Barbara Schwartz, Daniel Borzutzky, Jackie Clark, JC Hallman, Debbie Kuan, Jason Koo, Matt Shears, Garrett Caples, Johnny Schmidt, Anselm Berrigan, Matthew Rohrer, Gregory Crosby, & Dominique Townsend, & to my editor Richard Siken & co-publisher Drew Burk, who were instrumental in helping these poems achieve the forms found herein. Thanks to the following journals & newspapers who first published some of these poems, often in different forms: *Beloit Poetry Journal*, *Boog City*, *Epiphany*, *H_ngm_n*, *jubilat*, *Philadelphia Review of Books*, *Phoebe*, *Posit*, *Pretty Lit*, *Scapegoat Review*, & *Sink Review*. "The Poem" was first published as a pamphlet by Greying Ghost Press. "The Score" was written for a modern dance piece, *The Green Dance*, choreographed by Stephanie Sleeper for a SleepDance performance at Triskelion Arts in Williamsburg, Brooklyn; the poem took its first form as a pamphlet to accompany the dance. "The Journal" was republished in the Bowery Poetry Books' anthology *Poet Sculpture*, created & distributed by artist Sam Jablon for Art in Odd Places (AiOP). An earlier version of "Eth*OS" was republished on the Brooklyn Poets website. "Ode to the MQ-9 Reaper" was cited with lines quoted in *The New York Times*.

ABOUT THE AUTHOR

JOE PAN is the author of the poetry collections *Operating Systems, The Art Is a Lonely Hunter, Soffritto, Hi c cu ps*, and *Autobiomythography & Gallery*—five books in an ongoing series of autobiomythographies. He served as co-editor of the best-selling *Brooklyn Poets Anthology*, and his work has appeared in such venues as the *Boston Review, Hyperallergic, The New York Times*, and *The Philadelphia Review of Books*. He is publisher and editor-in-chief of Brooklyn Arts Press, an independent publishing house honored in 2016 with a National Book Award win in Poetry, as well as serving as the publisher of Augury Books, and is the founder of the services-oriented activist group Brooklyn Artists Helping.